Downstream

For Ross —
Thanks for sharing my love of good fishing
and good fishing stories!

DOWNSTREAM

Reflections on Brook Trout, Fly Fishing, and the Waters of Appalachia

DAVID L. O'HARA

and

MATTHEW T. DICKERSON

Foreword by Nick Lyons

Afterword by Bill McKibben

CASCADE *Books* · Eugene, Oregon

DOWNSTREAM
Reflections on Brook Trout, Fly Fishing, and the Waters of Appalachia

Cascade Books
An Imprint of Wipf and Stock Publishers
199 W. 8th Ave., Suite 3
Eugene, OR 97401

www.wipfandstock.com

ISBN 13: 978-1-62564-727-6

Cataloguing-in-Publication Data

O'Hara, David L., and Matthew T. Dickerson.

Downstream : reflections on brook trout, fly fishing, and the waters of Appalachia

xiv + 136 p. ; 23 cm. Includes bibliographical references.

ISBN 13: 978-1-62564-727-6

1. Fly fishing—Appalachia—United States. 2. Sports and recreation—fishing. 3.
Ecology—Appalachia—United States. I. Title.

SH 687 .O37 2014

Manufactured in the U.S.A.   07/31/2014

Contents

Foreword

ALL FISHING IS LOCAL. Every river is local, *sui generis*, its own unique combination of runs, riffles, pools, and flora, and aquatic life, and history, in a thousand configurations. Still, every river, every fishing experience, overlaps all others. Art Flick's Schoharie, Vince Marinaro's Letort, Roderick Haig-Brown's Campbell, and Harry Plunket Greene's unforgettable Bourne are personal to them but intensely interesting to anyone who fly fishes—for a host of reasons. Most of us will never fish those rivers; but any truly first-rate, thoughtful book like *Downstream*, with its measured exploration of particular Appalachian watersheds, will provide insights of immense value to the increasing army of fly fishers who fish the world over.

Here we have two splendid guides, both college professors, who seek wild brook trout from Maine to Georgia. They had fished some of these waters as youngsters and now fish them wisely and passionately and well, curious to understand and know the full allure of these waters and their wild denizens, where such still exist.

Matthew Dickerson and Dave O'Hara, each writing separate signed chapters, are great fishing pals and marvelous guides. They have written a book with modest aims—to understand more deeply waters they love, that are sometimes threatened, that still offer the anticipation and tangible rewards they seek from their fishing. Their fishing is well worth sharing but even more worthwhile are the steady observations about the heart of what they do, its links to all aspects of life away from rivers, its links to the emotions and friendship and a wise way to become part of the natural world. They are the farthest from, and decry, those who "bounce from one famous hole to the next, one river to another, even one state to another," ignorant of and never able to attain the intimacy they champion, the kind of knowledge that alone can lead to the protection of great wild waters.

Their book is full of enduring insights, vivid and memorable descriptions of where they've fished and what they've seen and learned. It is an intimate book. The fishing takes place in waters they especially want to fish, for the fish but also for the nature of the river, the locale, the history of the place. They explore the fishing and report sensibly about the great Androscoggin, the Little Tennessee, the Tellico, the South Holston, the Martin's Fork, the Mooselookmeguntic outlet, and dozens of other rivers, north and south, only some of which most of us have heard of. Always they seek wild brook trout, the canaries in the coal mine, the great symbol of piscatorial health and beauty. They find some, are disappointed when they find none, and look always for those unspoiled clean waters that such fish require.

Along the way, in a kind of Parsifalian quest, there is both an implicit and explicit eye for what despoils water that once held such fish, the specific ways in which such waters have been destroyed and what restoration has been undertaken, with what results.

"No matter where we live," they say, "our lives are made better by flowing water." *Downstream* in this sense is a paean for increased curiosity, for wiser understanding of that element that can surely make our lives better, and for more protection of this precious element. "We all live downstream from one another," they observe.

Possibility, anticipation, quietness, friendship, intimacy with the natural world, increased skills, and a love both spiritual and worldly—these qualities, which are often shared with the wisest practice of a religion, are qualities this fine book celebrates. All of our fishing may be local, but *Downstream* heralds virtues that all of us would be better to share.

—Nick Lyons

Acknowledgments

JUST AS A RIVER may have many headwaters that combine to feed the main stream, this book has come to life downstream of many influences and supporters. We are grateful to all the people and institutions who gave us their time and assistance as we researched and wrote this book. We have to take the blame for any errors, but much of the credit for what we got right belongs to others who helped us along the way.

We are especially grateful to the Oregon State University for the privilege of a two-week writing fellowship at Shotpouch Cabin in the mountains outside Corvallis in August 2012, and for the tremendous hospitality, encouragement, and feedback on our writing. We're likewise grateful to those who, like Charles Goodrich and Dave Lettero, maintain the Cabin and all it stands for. Every writer should have such opportunities, and such friends. If they did, the world would have many more good books.

Thanks to Middlebury College students Kelly March and Connor Wood (class of 2011), who worked with Matthew Dickerson in January 2009 to do research for this book in Tennessee and in Vermont. The maps that follow the Acknowledgments were created by Robert Seltzer (three regional maps of the Androscoggin River, various waters of Pennsylvania and New York, and the Holston and Cumberland Rivers) and Gregory Woolston (overview map of Appalachia), both undergraduate students at Middlebury College. Heartfelt thanks also to Jeff Howarth (Assistant Professor of Geography) for making the project possible by incorporating it into his cartography class and to Kat Schweikert (Assistant in Science Instruction of Geography) for helping prepare the data.

Acknowledgments

We're also grateful to:

Augustana College for ARAF grants, and Middlebury College (including the Palen Fund and the Ada Howe Kent fund), for supporting our research and writing during the summers of 2008–2012;

Kurt Fausch, for his decades of research and devotion to *S. fontinalis*; for his generosity in sharing that research with us and with his many students; and for his friendship and advice as we wrote;

Craig Spencer, for encouraging us to do this work, for the joy of teaching reef ecology with him in Belize, and for sharing his love of all things that flow;

Dan Howard, Carrie Hall, Steve Matzner, Amy Lewis, and the other members of the Augustana College Biology Department, for their helpful comments and for allowing Dave to haunt their department library and conference room, and for tolerantly allowing him to peer over their shoulders as they engaged in the serious and important work that they do so well;

Our guides and teachers, especially our Tennessee and Kentucky guides: Hagan Wonn, "Rocky" Cox, Mark Scarborough; and our guides in Maine: Mike Warren, and John and Nate Nichols;

Fishing buddies like Mike Burris, Al Bazinet, Bo Koeppen, and Dan Engebretson, who have shared the joy of moving water with us;

Steve Wrinn, for his generous advice and encouragement, in both writing and fishing;

Kathleen Dean Moore and John Elder, for setting the example of how to walk in rivers and woods with eyes open, feet shod with the readiness to feel whatever the river and woods bring, and a pen;

Nick Lyons, Bill McKibben, and Andrea Knutson for their encouragement with this project and their kind words of endorsement;

Our fathers, Almerin C. O'Hara and Willard Dickerson Jr., without whom we might never have found any other guides. They were our first guides and teachers; they brought us to the waters. Although we have now fished in more places and probably caught more fish than they have, every fish we have landed has been because of them, and to their credit;

And most of all, our saintly wives, Deborah and Christina, for all the times they let us go wandering in the mountains, and for understanding and supporting our love for beautiful, wonderful speckled trout.

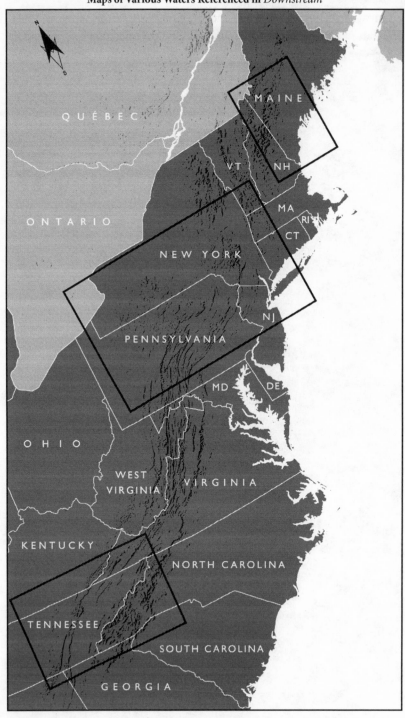

The Androscoggin River and Its Sources Referenced in *Downstream*

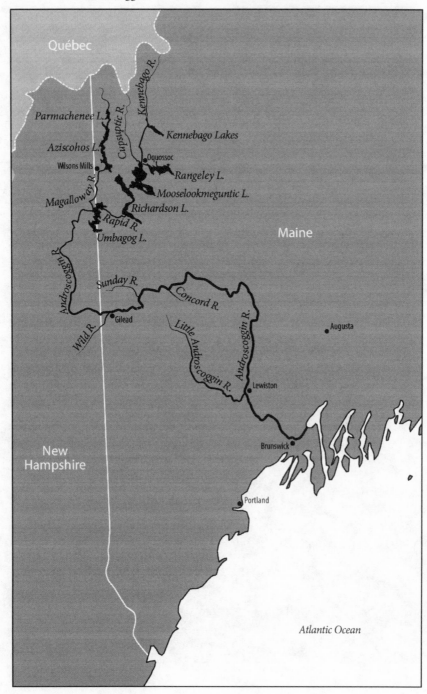

Waters of Pennsylvania and New York Referenced in *Downstream*

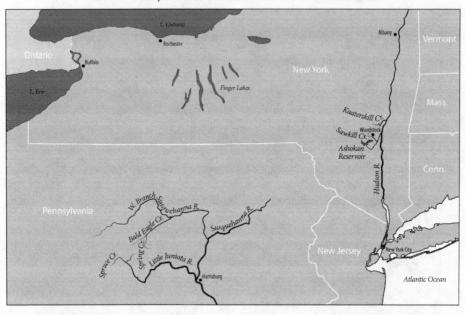

The Holston and Cumberland Rivers and Their Sources Referenced in *Downstream*

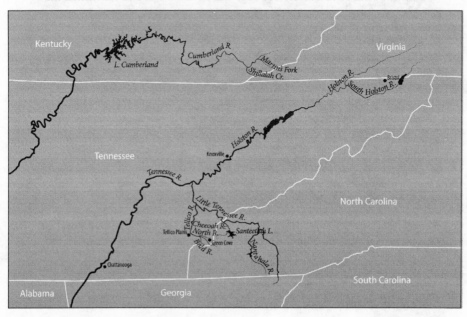

Introduction

Why We Write, and Why We Fish

There are two spiritual dangers in not owning a farm. One is the danger of supposing that breakfast comes from the grocery, and the other that heat comes from the furnace.

—Aldo Leopold

In 1940, novelist John Steinbeck set off on an expedition in the Gulf of California with his friend Ed Ricketts, a marine biologist. The ostensible purpose of their trip, he says, was "to observe the distribution of invertebrates, to see and to record their kinds and numbers, how they lived together, what they ate, and how they reproduced." But Steinbeck writes that those high-sounding activities and researches were only one of the reasons, and far from the real truth. The real reason, he says, is this: "we were curious." He then adds, "Our curiosity was not limited, but was as wide and horizonless as that of Darwin or Agassiz or Linnaeus or Pliny. We wanted to see everything our eyes would accommodate, to think what we could, and, out of our seeing and thinking, to build some kind of structure in modeled imitation of the observed reality." Elsewhere in the same chapter of his *Log from the Sea of Cortez,* Steinbeck writes that "the impulse which drives a man to poetry will send another man into the tide pools and force him to try to report what he finds there."

Our project—the project resulting in this book—was like theirs: we were curious, and we wanted to see everything we could.

1

We both grew up in the Appalachians, and as boys we learned to fish for trout in their waters. If we could explain simply why grown men are so fascinated with brook trout, or why we spend so much of our time waist-deep in their waters, soaked to the bone, shivering, and delighting in every encounter with a speckled trout, we wouldn't need to write stories. This book is the best answer we can give. The trout have drawn us into their waters, and we have come out of the waters with stories of what we have seen and learned. The more we fish, the more we find ourselves wanting to know, so that our pastime of fishing has grown into a subject of research. A few years ago, we started hiring guides who could take us to the waters they grew up in, and teach us what they knew. Over the last four or five years, we have looked for brook trout in nearly every Appalachian state, from Maine to Georgia, fishing numerous major watersheds and learning from anyone—fishing guides, government officials, wildlife biologists, hatchery workers, fellow fishers met at streamsides—willing to talk to us about fly fishing, Appalachia, and brook trout.

We have worked together to write this book, but we've each left our stamp on certain chapters. For a little while, we played with the idea of trying to come up with an anonymous voice, some third-person narrative or a generic "we" that belonged in some way to both of us, but in another way didn't belong to either one of us. We have, in the past, coauthored two published books using that approach. But those previous books were not about our own personal stories. At least not in the same direct way as is this book. In the end we decided to leave our chapters in the first person singular, and to leave our voices distinct and separate. We fish together, but we each hook and play our own fish, and our stories are like that, too. We have been walking together in these streams—both literal streams and streams of thought—for years, and we see a lot of things the same way. But we also see some things differently. Matthew is a Massachusetts native and a scientist, a novelist, an outdoors writer, who has lived in Maine and New Hampshire and now lives in Vermont, where he teaches creative writing, environmental studies, and computer science; Dave, born and raised in New York's Catskill Mountains, is a philosopher who now teaches environmental thought and American philosophy in South Dakota and reef ecology in Belize. Our experiences and our disciplines have guided our vision to slightly different objects, and have given different inflections to our voices. Even if the chapters of this book were not labeled with our names, we think it would become easy enough to determine which of us is writing.

Yet we also share a common vision, and we hope also that readers will see that, despite our different voices, we both care about the same things.

We've organized the book more or less geographically, beginning in the North and traveling south. Biologists tell us that brook trout most likely originated in the far North and journeyed south during periods of high water and glaciation. Not presuming to improve upon nature, we are following her example. We did, however, make an exception from southerly literary migration for the chapter whose story takes place in Kentucky, on the Cumberland River. We placed that chapter after our visit to Tennessee and the Holston for two reasons. One is that in Kentucky, unlike in every other state in the Appalachians, the native status of brook trout has been brought into question. The other reason has to do with hope. Our chapter on the Holston and the restoration of wild southern brook trout in its headwaters is a story full of hope. Our chapter on Kentucky, by contrast, runs a bit darker, just as the rivers there are silted by runoff from mountaintop removal. Though we are unwilling to pass over the less pleasant stories of our beloved Appalachians, we prefer good news, and like to give it pride of place.

Our first chapter looks at trout in Maine, and the mixed record of human modifications of fisheries there. The second chapter focuses on New York and Pennsylvania, and the ways knowledge of these waters gets passed on from one generation to the next. Our third and fourth chapters bring us to some of the peculiar and fascinating waters of the central Appalachians. The third chapter visits waters that straddle Kentucky and Tennessee. Kentucky is the only Appalachian state that makes the official claim that it has no indigenous brook trout, a claim about which we admit some skepticism. Kentucky also boasts one of the best big-water trout rivers in the East, all of it due to human modification of the environment. Perhaps surprisingly to anyone who thinks of brook trout as northern fish, the last few chapters focus on southern brook trout. Our final chapter brings us to the beautifully contemplative Smoky Mountains of North Carolina and Tennessee and our quest for the indigenous southern strain of brook trout.

At this point our alert readers will note the omission of stories taking them to New Hampshire, Massachusetts, New Jersey, Maryland, West Virginia, Georgia, or South Carolina. Even Vermont, where Matthew lives and where he and David first began fishing together, gets only scant attention in this book. Yet all of these states lay good claim to being Appalachian.

This omission is neither one of mere oversight, nor lack of geographic knowledge on the part of the authors. It certainly does not come from lack of interest, as all of these states have some good trout waters where the authors have fished, or would like to fish. Even the relatively small state of New Jersey has some beautiful wild brook trout water, especially up in the Delaware Water Gap area. It is merely a practical result of the limitations of time and space, and the costs of publishing. Perhaps in our next book we will redress this wrong.

In addition to allowing ourselves some glaring omissions, and some variations in our southerly course, we've also allowed ourselves a literary conceit of appending a coda to each chapter, as a sort of dam, a reflective pause or watery "selah" separating one watershed from the next. The book of Genesis records that this was one of God's first acts, "separating the waters below from the waters above." Genesis adds, "and it was very good." We're not so sanguine about the impoundments we put on waterways, many thousands of which exist in the waters of Appalachia. Hydroelectric dams, flood control dams, splash dams, channelization and dikes, fish ladders—we humans do a lot of separation of waters from waters, and all of these things affect the trout. One of our main ideas is that what affects trout usually affects the whole watershed; and what affects the watershed affects everything, and everyone, that lives downstream. These little literary "dams" serve to remind us of this. Dams on rivers do some harm, but they also often make places where moving water sits still a while, places of both literal and metaphorical reflection. In the same way, our pauses between chapters are attempts to still our narrative and to give us a chance to reflect a bit more abstractly on some of what we've learned from the trout and the rivers we fish. Even so, as much as we've enjoyed writing them, we're always glad to see fish find ways over or around dams, and if you feel like skipping them to get back to our narratives, go right ahead.

We probably could have done all our research at home, using the library and the Internet. We've gathered enough scientific papers, historical articles, technical books and guides on trout and Appalachia that we could have written this without ever going into the mountains. But if we had to choose between fishing without writing and writing without fishing, we'd definitely choose the first. The trout of the Appalachians are not primarily a topic of research for us. They are, as we have already noted, the fish we grew up with; they are a kind of canary in a coal mine that show us how our watersheds are doing; and they are not, in the end, the only thing we're interested in. Sometimes you can only see what you don't look at directly, by unfocusing your gaze. The rhythm of casting a fly rod breaks the habitual rhythms of modern life for us, disrupting our busy thoughts like a Zen koan. Fishing for trout requires us to try to see the world as trout see it, to imagine their riparian cosmos, in which everything is connected, everything flows together, and the aim is to find your place in that flow. The ancient Greek philosopher Thales said, "All is water." He must have been thinking like a trout. At any rate, when we try to think like a trout, and we make contact, something new comes into being, a relationship and an experience for which we cannot imagine substituting research. Once again, Steinbeck says it well in describing his research:

> We knew that what we would see and record and construct would be warped, as all knowledge patterns are warped, first, by the collective pressure and stream of our time and race, second by the thrust of our individual personalities. But knowing this, we might not fall into too many holes—we might maintain some balance between our warp and the separate thing, the external reality. The oneness of these two might take its contribution from both. For example: the Mexican sierra has "XVII-15-IX" spines in the dorsal fin. These can easily be counted. But if the sierra strikes hard on the line so that our hands are burned, if the fish sounds and nearly escapes and finally comes in over the rail, his colors pulsing and his tail beating the air, a whole new relational externality has come into being—an entity which is more than the sum of the fish plus the fisherman.[1]

Like Steinbeck, we set out to do some research. But that was only the ostensible reason. Once again, we were curious. We were curious about that "whole new relational externality" that might come into being. We are not content simply to know these waters by reading about them. We wanted to know them as one can only know by standing in them, patiently petitioning their inhabitants through slow repetitions of cast and retrieval, and through sustained observation and conversation. This book flows out of the time we have spent doing just that. We hope it will bring you some pleasure, and maybe help you get to know your own waters a bit better, too.

Chapter 1

Tracing the Androscoggin
The Resurrection of a River

Matthew Dickerson

I think of feelings I have had when stopping my car on a cross country drive in the desert and standing there in the windy loneliness for a while, hearing nothing, seeing shadows, the subtle color differences in different heights and textures of blowing grasses, feeling the extreme largeness of the outdoor room and its horizonless walls; or I think of the feeling of waking up in the musty woods with daylight barely filtering through motionless leaves overhead, the dampness on the ground felt as an unheard thud; or the smell of piñon wood burning, and the cold air carrying it into my nostrils, as the sun drapes red dirt and rocks with the crimson curtain of a melancholy sunset. . . . The primacy of these feelings impels me to capture them, and preserve them in my memory forever; to conjure the magic of something good waiting around the corner, over the hill, tomorrow, on the morning of the resurrection.

—Mark Heard, "Life in the Industry: a Musician's Diary"

IT IS MID-MORNING ON a late June day when we arrive in the tiny village of Gilead, Maine and put our canoe into the Androscoggin River. We park the car at the bridge downstream from the small delta where the Wild River flows in from the south out of Evans Notch and the shadow of Mount Washington. It is a rich and verdant valley. The shores are lined with a varied mix of hardwoods and conifers. Tall pines and spruce tower over the smaller cedars right on the water's edge. The white of the occasional paper birch stands in sharp contrast to the deeper greens. Standing here I think of the biblical town of Gilead in another mountainous region, one east of the Jordan River in ancient Israel. The name Gilead means "hill of witness." This modern Gilead, also, will be a witness of something good, of life where there once was death. It will be a place of balm to heal an old and mortal wound.

Dave and I are here with Dave's thirteen-year-old son, Michael, for a day of fly fishing and canoeing along a six-mile-long float of the Androscoggin. In the past, the river has held transplanted European browns and west coast rainbows. But recently native eastern brookies have been returning—some on their own, finding their way down from clean mountain tributaries like the Wild River, and some with the help of state hatchery trucks. We are hoping to hook some brook trout, but we will be happy to catch any trout at all.

To say that the water is high, however, would be a gross understatement. Two weeks of daily thunderstorms have turned it into a dark and wild torrent. "Almost unfishable" is the expression we use to describe it. And dark clouds are threatening even more rain. We consider turning back to the camp where we are staying twenty minutes away in the village of Bryant Pond. But Dave and Michael have driven from South Dakota to spend a week with me in Maine. We don't have the luxury of waiting a few days for the water to settle. So we go through the motions of setting up our rods and tying on flies, even though this small labor may prove futile.

Just below its confluence with the Wild River, the main current of the Androscoggin divides around a wide gravel bar. The stronger current flows down the southern shore past a pair of huge granite boulders, deposited here centuries ago by the forces that shape rivers. A few dozen yards below the boulders, the river narrows and the southern channel swirls hard around a long, deep ledge. A smaller channel, though one still too deep to wade except in midsummer, follows the wooded northern shore. The gravel bar separating these two channels is about thirty yards wide and fifty yards long. In the summer it typically ranges from a few inches deep to something just over the knees. When the water is at midsummer low, some of the gravel bar becomes exposed, and the currents on either side are slow and shallow enough that a steady and adventurous wader can sometimes work out to it from upstream. On the downstream side, however, it drops off into a deep hole and is accessible only by boat.

My favorite way to fish this stretch is to canoe up from below, anchor the canoe on rocks or in shallow water midstream between the swift currents, and then step out of the canoe and wade the gravel bar in the middle of the river. In this way I can cast to either side or work the deep pool below without having to deal with the clumsiness of casting from a canoe.

On this day, however, this gravel bar is under so much water it isn't even visible. Not that it matters. We couldn't paddle a canoe against the heart of the rain-swelled current. There is no way up there without an outboard motor. And no anchor would hold us even if we succeeded in getting there. The best we can do is paddle hard up the eddies against the north shore and take a few casts behind the boulders that stick out a dozen yards downstream of the gravel bar. Dave is in the bow of our canoe, and Michael sits in a low seat in the middle. I am in the stern. Dave and Michael tie on streamers, and I put on a large heavily weighted stonefly nymph. We make the requisite casts, letting our flies sink as deep as they can. The casts, as expected, are fruitless. We should probably remove the word "almost" from the phrase "almost unfishable." The turbulent water is the color of tea that has been left steeping far too long. Perhaps Earl Grey, Dave's favorite afternoon blend. How many feet of visibility in a really large cup of Earl Grey?

It is time to make a mental transition. I have to stop thinking of this as a day of fishing, and think of it instead as a six-mile canoe trip in swift water, during which I might make a few casts. If I think of it as fishing trip, I will be disappointed. If I think of it as a canoe trip perhaps I can enjoy the scenery and not be bothered by a lack of fish. I turn the canoe out of the eddy into the current, clutch at the sides for that brief moment of panic as the swift rush of water catches us broadside, and then start downstream for a six-mile paddle.

From Gilead to West Bethel where we will take out, the Androscoggin is a braided river full of long narrow wooded islands. There are usually two channels to choose from, and often three or occasionally even four. Steep bluffs and ledges rise on the north side, providing continuous reminders that we are in the Appalachians; it is really more of a cut through a pass in the hills than a valley. A more potent reminder comes less frequently, when the river rounds a bend at just the right angle to afford a glimpse, looking back upstream, of the presidential range of the White Mountains. Washington, Adams, and Jefferson, the highest peaks in the northeast, rise about fifteen miles to the west, though in this high flooded water there is not much time for looking around at them. The moment we pass under the bridge and out of the catch-and-release single-hook regulation stretch of river, we are faced with a choice of braids. We choose the one on the right.

At the next bend in the river downstream from the bridge, we come to what is usually a small gravel island dotted with a few bushes. It is a favorite spot to beach the canoe and cast from the shore. On this day, however, the island is thigh-deep under water, marked only by the bushes sticking up and bending in the current. There is no shore on which to pull up our canoe. Still, the sunken island is a place we might be able to wade. We paddle the canoe into the V-shaped eddy behind the island, drop the anchor, and clamber out into the bushes and the thigh-deep water.

Brook trout have lived in this watershed for millennia. Time without count the population has survived the mild flood conditions of ordinary spring rains or heavy August thunderstorms. Brown and rainbow trout, though recent additions to the local ecosystem, also have the right survival instincts. In this dark and turbulent water, they usually hug the bottom of the river, or hold in the eddies behind rocks and islands out of the current. The rain has almost certainly washed a fair amount of food into the river, but it will be difficult for the fish to see that food. This provides both the challenge and the opportunity for anglers in conditions like this: to add our artificial fare to the natural buffet floating past in such a way that we get our offering to where the fish are hiding out, close enough that they can see it. We search our fly boxes for flies that will sink as deep as possible, and be as visible as possible. I tie on the largest and heaviest light-colored nymph I can find in my vest. It is an imitation of a golden stonefly with a shiny bead as its head. To add to my remote chance of hooking a fish I tie a foot and a half of tippet to the bend on the hook of the stonefly and at the end of that tippet add on a second fly: a smaller bead-head hare's ear. The larger and heavier fly helps get the offering down deeper in the current, and with any luck attracts the attention of the fish. The smaller fly may appear more realistic or more edible, or just less gaudy. It is also a way to try two fly patterns imitating different foods at the same time in hopes that at least one will be appealing.

Anglers are always making trade-offs when fly fishing. One trade-off has to do with the size of the tippet: the last bit of leader at the end of the line, connected to the fly. Lighter tippet is less visible, and thus less likely to spook a fish. Smaller flies and clear water and cautious fish all require lighter tippet. Unfortunately, lighter tippet is also weaker. It breaks more easily. Bigger flies, or less clear water, allow heavier, stronger tippet. When fishing two nymphs at the same time, the lower one is called a dropper. Droppers are also tied on with lighter tippet than the upper fly. There are two reasons for doing this. First, if the leader does not taper down in size toward the end, it is harder to cast it properly; lighter tippet at the end helps the leader to roll over and land the fly gently on the surface with the line fully straightened out. Second, if the dropper gets caught on a rock or log or other snag, a lighter tippet at the end means the dropper breaks off more easily without the upper fly also breaking off. Losing one fly is not as bad as losing two.

My dropper breaks off almost at once as I try to bump it along the bottom where I think the fish are. I make a mental note that I should have switched to stronger leader. In this murky water, trout are not going to see even the heaviest leader. For that matter, how are the trout even going to see my fly?

In a moment of inspiration or desperation, I remember a large, heavy, white bead-headed long-tailed wooly bugger with red hackle my friend Wes Butler had recently tied for me. It is not tied to imitate one particular thing. Drifted along the current, it might look like a big leech floating downstream. Pulled through the water with quick twitches, it might look like a small fish. Most important to me, right now, it might be the only fly I have that is big and bright enough for trout to see in this water. I tie it on and wade back to the "V" at the tail end of the island. I stand behind the anchored canoe and take a few casts over the bushes, alternating between sides. With each cast I strip out more line, putting my fly farther out into the swift current, and letting the river haul it farther downstream.

Even when fish are not biting, I find it soothing and healing to stand in water. It is a balm for my soul. And it is also invigorating—as well as adrenaline-raising—to stand in water so swift it threatens to pull me off my feet if I am not careful. With a rod in hand and a fly in the water, I can feel the pulse and vibration of the current as it tugs on my line and fly, just as I feel it pull on my feet and legs. That feel is important not only for sensing the strike of a fish, but even for sensing the movement of the fly: the bounce of a heavy nymph along the rocky bottom of a river, or the swirls and tugs of a streamer fly darting in the current like a small baitfish. Or, when things are going well, the sudden stop in movement of that drifting fly as a trout sucks it in. These are the indications, sometimes subtle, that I need to lift my rod and set a hook. Dave and I are both musicians, and the thrum and pulse of water over line reminds us a little of the soothing feel of a guitar in our hands. We not only hear the music, but we can feel the vibration of the flattop soundboard beneath our fingertips, or against our thighs and chest.

Bang! To my stunned amazement I feel a hard hit. I lift my rod smoothly but swiftly and tug back. The hook is set. The line is no longer a connection to water only. The dance has begun. The fish pulls hard. Each dart of the tail, each toss of its head, sends a pulse up the line, through the rod, to the hands that hold the rod. A minute later I land a healthy fish. It is only ten inches long, but the swift, near-flood-stage current made it feel half again bigger than that. More important to me than its size, however, is its species. It is not just an imported and stocked brown or rainbow trout, as we had been expecting, but a wild brook trout.

DEATH AND RESURRECTION

As I noted, Gilead is a fortuitous name for this village where we now fish. The town is more than just a witness. A traditional spiritual first sung by African-American slaves before the Civil War begins with the lines, "There is a balm in Gilead, / To make the wounded whole; / There's power enough in heaven, / To cure a sin-sick soul." This hymn might well have been sung about Gilead, Maine and the Androscoggin River.

A glimpse into the history of the Androscoggin River is a glimpse at the importance of the brook trout that took a white wooly bugger on rain-swollen water on a late June day. I spent much of my life in and around this part of western Maine. In the fall of 1968, I went to kindergarten in the village of Bryant Pond, just a few miles from the larger ski town of Bethel, where the Androscoggin River takes a big bend northward on its journey from the mountains to the sea. My family has had a cottage in Bryant Pond for more than four decades. I learned to fish on many of the smaller local streams that feed the Androscoggin, including not only the Wild River but also lesser-known streams like the Little Androscoggin River, Concord River, and Alder Brook. These were the streams where I cut my fishing teeth. Streams where I first learned to read the water; to cast first a worm, and then a lure, and then a fly; to bushwhack around swamps and sneak up on deep holes; and where I first practiced thinking like a trout, or thinking like I thought a trout would think. In all of them, even the smallest, I can still picture certain holes where I caught trout, or hoped to catch trout, or lost trout. To this day, when I drive past one of these streams (which is quite often) I have some flash of nostalgic memory.

Two of my favorite rivers in this area were Sunday River and Bear River—both long, tumbling, cascading, wandering, gravelly, swift cold mountain streams flowing off the southwest and northwest bowls of Old Speck, the third highest mountain in Maine. Lower down on these rivers was the land of stocked rainbows. But if I went far enough up Sunday River, hiking or following the old gravel logging roads, or if I worked into the upper portions of Bear River and the little creeks that tumble off the sides of Grafton Notch to feed it, I could get into some good wild brook trout water. Even lower down, the water was clear and cold and clean enough to support brook trout as well as rainbows, though the latter dominated. In those days—before Sunday River became one of the biggest ski resorts in the east, and development hit the valley like the leading wave of a failed dam—the Bear and the Sunday rivers were pristine waters, and I felt like I was really in the wilderness when I fished them. I could spend all day on upper Sunday River and not see another person or hear a single car.

The Androscoggin River, by contrast, was something different. When I was living in Maine in the late 1960s, and later on throughout the 1970s when I returned to the area for summer vacations, I would not even have canoed the Androscoggin, much less fished it or swum in it. The river was beyond vile. It was full of trash, poisoned by the legal dumping of industrial waste from paper mills, and fouled by household toilets that dumped raw sewage right into the river. The sewage could be seen floating down the river, if one had the stomach to look into the water. In *The Lord of the Rings*, when Tolkien's heroes Frodo and Sam first glimpse the Land of Mordor, inhabited by the demonic foe Sauron and his legions of orcs and trolls, the narrator describes the scene through the hobbits' eyes:

> Here nothing lived, not even the leprous growths that feed on rottenness. The gasping pools were choked with ash and crawling muds, sickly white and grey, as if the mountains had vomited the filth of their entrails upon the lands about. . . . [It was] a land defiled, diseased beyond all healing—unless the Great Sea should enter in and wash it with oblivion.[2]

This would have been an apt description of the Androscoggin as it flowed through Bethel. Except it was not the mountains that had vomited their entrails; it was the lumber mills and factories and human cities.

Hard as it might be to believe, once the Androscoggin left the Appalachians and hit the farmlands downstream of Bethel, it got even worse as it picked up runoff from industrialized agriculture: pesticides, herbicides, and chemical fertilizer, in addition to the manure and the mud from fast-eroding soils that are inevitable in heavily tilled lands. Rumford, twenty some miles downstream of Bethel, was yet another paper mill town glad to use the river as its sewer and chemical disposal system. In 1972, *Time* magazine listed the Androscoggin River as one of the ten filthiest rivers in the entire United States. Nobody who lived near it had cause to doubt that ranking.

That was over forty years ago. It has been a few years since I have caught trout in Sunday River. That small mountain stream has taken a noticeable downturn in beauty and quality, thanks to development associated with a major ski industry. But during that same period there has been an incredible resurrection of the Androscoggin upstream of where Sunday River flows in. This resurrection of the Androscoggin started in the 1970s, thanks in large part to the now famous Clean Water Act of 1972. The restoration was no sudden Easter morning event. It took many years to achieve. It was not until the late 1990s that I first dared to wade in the Androscoggin, just below the confluence of the Wild River in Gilead a few miles downstream of the New Hampshire border. Though I had been hearing for a couple years about the river's restoration, that restoration was difficult to imagine and to accept, knowing what I did of the river's history and the defiled state it had been in just a couple decades earlier; it was difficult to bring myself to put a canoe into its waters, or cast a fly there. But when I finally stood in the water, it really did seem miraculous. It did feel like Easter morning. I wonder how many others, who remember the water from forty years ago, felt that way when they woke up one morning realizing what had happened.

So there I had stood, a decade before my canoe trip with David and Michael, wading the Androscoggin for the first time. On that earlier visit I was with my father and one of my sons. It was a beautiful early summer day. The air was scented with pine and spruce and especially cedar, and with the delightful and unique aroma of a large forest river—the sort of tumbling, well-aerated river that always carries the rich red-brown tint of decaying leaves even when running clear and clean. The clean smell, familiar to me from dozens of rivers I have fished, and refreshing as it conjures thoughts of trout in a way no other smell does, was also startling given what that same spot would have smelled like forty years ago. What was the scent of an open tomb on Easter morning?

On that earlier occasion, after casting for a time where we put in, we'd also spent the rest of the day canoeing and fishing the stretch downstream from Gilead. It is just the right distance from Gilead to the take-out in Bethel for an afternoon and evening of fishing. It would be a short afternoon for canoeists who kept their paddles in the water and did not stop for picnics. But for the angler who frequently drops anchor or pulls to shore to wade, or simply drifts at a slow pace and takes time to cast, it can easily fill the hours from lunch to sunset. There is plenty to enjoy beyond the good fishing, too. In addition to the majestic views of the Presidential Range occasionally opening up in the upstream direction, we had several sightings of bald eagles, blue heron, osprey, and kingfishers, all feeding on an abundant supply of food in the water. In the evening, we paddled through one of the thickest hatches of caddis flies I have seen east of the Mississippi River. The rising fish made us smile, but we had to smile carefully, with our mouths closed, to keep ourselves from dining on the same insect meal the trout were eating.

We also landed several fish. Just in the short stretch from the gravel bar to the first bend below the bridge we caught numerous rainbow trout, one brown trout, a landlocked salmon, and a bass. The rainbows and browns had been stocked there by the state, in response to the complete turnaround of the quality of that water. They were fat, and strong, and fun to catch. That day, the river fished like a blue-ribbon trout stream. The once-fouled water was now clean again, and we had no qualms about putting our hands in it to release the fish we had caught.

But on that day also it was the smallest fish we caught that left us most excited: a brook trout of maybe eleven inches in length, a native lover of clean cold water and a prime indication of the health of an Appalachian watershed. The tone of its skin was a deep rich green, and its spots so bright red and yellow they looked painted on. Hatchery fish, living in crowded raceways and feeding on a bland, unchanging diet of pellets, lack the vibrant colors of their wild relatives. We have seen enough pale and pasty stocked fish to know when we have caught one. This one was wild. It, or its ancestors, had presumably found its own way down from some high tributary, and was once more thriving in water its relatives had long ago inhabited. It was the clearest sign we could have hoped for that this river was alive again. There is, indeed, a balm in Gilead to cure a sin-sick soul. Or a sin-sick river.

BROOK TROUT MECCA

And here I find myself again, a decade later, fishing with Dave's son Michael and holding a wild brook trout. Even through the Earl Grey water, the red and yellow circles set against that dark green skin of this char are beautiful to look at. It is easy to see why some native peoples thought of the fish as sacred. Keeping the wild brook trout in the water as much as possible, I gently remove the hook while admiring its beauty. I hold it under the water and stroke it for just a moment, and then release it to swim off.

The fish is not alone. Over the next few minutes I catch one more brookie, plus a rainbow. When I invite Michael to join me, he hooks and lands a fat rainbow. The fish are densely packed into this little lee. Here they are protected from the raging current, and they are hungry. Sitting inside the "V" they can get to food floating by on both sides, but they don't have to swim in the strong current. These fish know where to go in a flood.

Unfortunately, they would be the only fish we would catch on the entire drift—though after I leave the canoe and hitchhike my way back up to Gilead to grab our car, Dave manages to complete the cycle of trout genera by catching a brown trout, bringing our combined total for the day to five fish. It is better than we expected. So the "almost" in "almost unfishable" was needed after all.

Three days later we are dozens of miles and several large lakes upstream. We are on the Kennebago River just below Little Kennebago Lake, with Maine guides John and Nate Nichols. After our day on the flooded Androscoggin, Dave, Michael, and I spent the next two and a half days leapfrogging our way up the watershed. We spent a day and a half on Rapid River, the most remote of all the stretches of river we would fish in the Androscoggin watershed, and probably the most famous. It is the place where Louise Dickinson Rich "took to the woods," and in 1942 published a book about her experience there. We'd also spent a morning at Upper Dam and an afternoon far upstream on the Kennebago River above Little Kennebago Lake. Up there, the Kennebago River is really just a stream, much too small even for a kayak, although a fitting home for a species of trout with "brook" in its name.

I've been going to Rapid River for more than twenty years, mostly with my brother Ted, and I've caught a lot of hefty and healthy landlocked salmon and brook trout there. However, Dave and I had been in there together only once before, many years earlier. The previous experience was almost exactly opposite in one way—it was during a summer when the water was especially low, and thus also rather warm. We hadn't done very well on that earlier trip, and fishing was no better this time, although for the opposite reason: Rapid River was in the same watershed and weather system as the Androscoggin and had received the same rains. It was running at almost that same "almost unfishable" level of near-flood. I had managed to catch just one brook trout and one landlocked salmon over a day and a half of fishing.

By contrast we had hit Upper Dam just right. Whatever powers were in charge of such things had closed some gates on the dam thanks to two consecutive days without rain, and the lowering water brought some fish in. We all caught several brookies over fifteen inches in length, mostly on streamers. It was the best trout fishing Michael had ever had, which made it very memorable for his father as well as for Michael.

Now, however, we are on the Kennebago, a much smaller river than the Androscoggin, carrying just a fraction of the flow that passes through Upper Dam or down the Rapid River. To get to the lake, we drove several miles north from the village of Oquossoc up a dirt road toward a place where we are supposed to meet our guides. These Maine lumber roads are unmarked and can be confusing. Their purpose is to access lumber, not fishing. The loggers who work them every day know exactly where they are going, and they don't need signs. We, by contrast, would very much have liked some signs. I am reminded that most of northern Maine is still lumber country, much of it owned by big paper companies, though some is still owned by smaller entities, by the state, or by conservation groups. Historically, most of Maine's interior was shaped by the lumber business. This is evident when you look at any small town in northern or western Maine. As late as 1968 the little village of Bryant Pond had not just one but two active mills on its namesake lake. One made wooden clothespins, and the other made wooden spools to hold sewing thread. Today, both are closed. One was demolished and replaced by summer homes. The other was turned into lakeside condos. The Penley Corporation, in the neighboring village of West Paris, made wooden matchsticks from locally lumbered wood. Last time I saw a box of Penley strike-anywhere matches they were imported from China.

Most of the mills in this part of the state, like the Penley mill that opened in 1923 and was finally shut down in 2002, are gone now. But the industry left its mark on the land and water as well as on the people and culture. Just as the Androscoggin had been slowly poisoned to death by the paper industry, many Maine rivers that had been trophy brook trout waters, or had held incredible runs of prized Atlantic salmon, were also ruined by the profitable logging business which, in part, helped supply the paper business. Some smaller streams were destroyed by erosion caused by the building of logging roads and heavy cutting of trees. Some larger rivers were killed because they were used as the easiest way to float massive quantities of logs downriver, and the acid in the wood, the bark, and other debris poisoned the water and buried the bottom. Still other rivers were dramatically and negatively impacted by dams that cut off trout from spawning grounds and slowed the rivers, silting over the rocky bottoms.

Shockingly, some rivers were even intentionally poisoned to death when loggers dumped oil into them to kill the black flies. When we learned this fact, it left a pit in our stomachs. Amidst all the unintentional or collateral damage done to rivers by the logging and paper industries, what haunts me the most is thinking about somebody intentionally sterilizing a wild Maine river. The oil killed not just the black flies it was intended to kill but also the mayflies and caddis flies, the dragonflies and stoneflies, the crayfish and salamanders, as well as many birds and other critters that eat them. This, of course, includes the brook trout. And yet, having been in the Maine woods during black fly season, it is at least possible to feel some sympathy toward the loggers who had no choice but to be in the woods. I have more than once been driven out of the Maine woods by black flies so bad that there was no fishing worth the suffering they induced—black flies that crawl in the nose and ears and eyes, that leave you dripping blood on the neck or behind the wrists. It is a memory almost as haunting as the oil in the river.

Decades later, many of these rivers, like the Androscoggin, have recovered to some degree. As the waters became cleaner, many insect populations have reestablished themselves, and have been followed by other creatures higher up the food chain. Trout populations recovered, or found their way back from connected waters, or were restocked. Logging

17

practices have gotten healthier and more environmentally friendly, at least in the Northeast. Or, in many places, logging has just become so unprofitable it has stopped. The road network is still there, though all but the major arteries are somewhat organic and always shifting depending on the needs of the loggers. We are reminded that the roads, like dams, are there for purposes other than the fishing. But the result—the by-product of the need for wood and for power—is convenient for us anglers.

We are also reminded that these roads are still active lumber roads. Coming around a corner, we are forced to stop and wait for fifteen minutes while a massive piece of modern logging equipment processes a pile of trees. One claw picks a mature spruce off the pile as though it were no more than a toothpick and swings it over to the stripping machine. There, with one swift and violent rip, the once-living tree is denuded of all its branches and greenery and most of its bark. Then in the blink of an eye and with eerie and almost silent ease, a Skilsaw on steroids drops down and slices the top off. Presumably the wood above this point is not valuable, but it is still a diameter large enough it would have taken me half a minute to cut with my chainsaw. We realize the incredible power in the machinery we are watching. It is incredible human engineering, too. Some creative person designed that machine. Only later would we learn its name: delimber. How quickly it is possible, with our modern technology, to delimb and deforest the world.

Eventually, we make it to our destination: a bridge over the Kennebago River, a mile or so upstream of Kennebago Lake, and just two bends and maybe two hundred yards downstream of Little Kennebago Lake. Standing on the bridge and looking upriver, we can see small brook trout rising all across the water. It is a good sign, and anticipation is high as we unload the canoes and put them in at the bridge with the plan of paddling upstream to the Little Kennebago Lake. John Nichols takes Dave and Michael in his made-in-Maine Old Town canoe. Nate, wearing a green Red Sox cap emblazoned with a bright red *B*, takes me. It is a gorgeous late June afternoon. The rain has finally stopped. The air is pleasant. Mosquitoes are out, as they usually are in June, but not yet in full force. The air temperature and possibility of mosquitoes prompts us to put on long sleeves. Soon after we start paddling, the long sleeves feel overwarm and we roll them up. Once on the open water, the mosquitoes disappear anyway.

We catch one or two small trout right before we even start up the river, but the guides assure us we want to move up to bigger water. "There are big brookies in this lake," John tells us. "Some four and five pounders are caught at the inlet every fall when they gather to spawn."

That is enough motivation. Since we have to get upriver, we help the guides paddle up the slow current, around to the right, and slowly back to the left, and out toward the open flat water of Little Kennebago Lake. A pair of fly casters stand wading in chest-deep water at the outlet of the lake. We skirt to the side to avoid disturbing them and watch one land a fish. We then head out and around the lake, working the western shoreline, casting streamers en route to the far side and the inlet where the Kennebago River enters the lake. We can see across to the eastern shore, which has a small cluster of fishing cabins. We think how nice it would be to stay in one and be on the lake during a really good hatch, or in the fall when the lunker brook trout are moving. "That spot will be lined with fishermen when the big trout start to spawn," John tells us, as if reading our thoughts. On this evening, though, we have almost the whole lake to ourselves. Other than the two anglers we passed on the way into the lake, our only company is a pair of loons working the north end, and one other canoe with a pair of anglers paddling along the eastern shore. Now and then one of the loons pauses and lets out its mournful cry. It carries across the lake and bounces off the hills, echoing back before the original sound has ceased. We pause and listen, enraptured by the setting.

Late afternoon is turning to early evening when we reach the far side of the lake in our pair of canoes. There, Dave and Michael stop with their guide John and fish around the river mouth, while Nate and I paddle and fish our way upstream for several minutes and many bends in the channel, exploring the river itself until the current and the depth make it too difficult to continue. Then we turn and drift slowly down, and I fish through the stretch even more carefully while Nate handles the paddle and makes sure we don't get back to the lake too quickly. The river has a nice gravel bottom, with a few scattered boulders. The banks are lined with brush. Brook trout soon start rising regularly along the steep banks. Below the brush. Behind rocks. In the riffs. Everywhere. I switch from a streamer to a dry fly imitating a caddis and I start catching wild brookies almost as quickly as I can cast.

The number of brook trout in the river is incredible. I catch twenty in the first hour, and then I stop counting. They are small, wild, native brook trout. None bigger than twelve inches. But they are abundant! And they are a pure strain. This lake, unlike many Maine lakes further south, has never been stocked. Because of the natural barriers downstream between Little Kennebago Lake and any water that has ever been stocked, it is believed that no introduced brook trout has ever made it into these waters. I have been told that when the state of Maine wants to get some pure, northern strain wild brook trout, unbastardized by previous stockings, this is where they come. I can see why.

We can also see why the river is able to support such a healthy population of fish. The rocks are covered with caddis larvae. We get some photos of rocks covered with caddis casings. Later we look at the photos and count the larvae. There are more than fifty clinging to a patch of one rock no bigger than a square yard. This is excellent trout habitat. Clean, cold water, good canopy, plenty of food, and an undiluted strain of *S. fontinalis*. After catching enough small trout to feed an army—and keeping two for supper—I return back down to the lake. The sun is just dipping behind the near ridgeline. Sunset will be in an hour or so. Time to paddle back down to the cars.

SHARING THE RIVER

It is eleven months later, in May 2009, that Dave and I find ourselves back in the region. My nephew Michael, at the time a student at Middlebury College, has joined us. Seven years earlier, as a thirteen-year-old, Michael was already tying flies professionally for a local fly shop in western North Carolina, and reading fly-tying magazines. It was Michael's father, my brother Ted, who first introduced me to fishing in this region in the late 1980s. Now I am introducing Michael. We are on the Magalloway River, another of the major mountain headwater tributaries of the upper Androscoggin.

There are numerous tributaries that ultimately feed the Androscoggin River. These include the Cupsuptic, the Kennebago, and the Rangeley rivers, which feed it through Mooselookmeguntic Lake and Upper Dam, along with smaller tributaries like the Swift Cambridge and the Dead Cambridge rivers, which flow into Umbagog Lake along with Rapid River. Of all these, the Magalloway could lay the best claim to being the "Upper Androscoggin." The Magalloway ends at the western edge of Umbagog Lake. It doesn't even really flow into the lake. It slows down into some backwater channels that are home to moose, bald eagles, blue heron, and countless waterfowl. Then, gathering the water of Umbagog Lake and all the other tributaries feeding it, it emerges from these channels as the Androscoggin.

Our first stop on the Magalloway is in the little village of Wilson Mills, Maine, just a half dozen miles upstream of the New Hampshire border, and only a dozen miles upstream of where the Magalloway officially becomes the Androscoggin. Like most of the rivers in the region, and even some of the ponds and portions of lakes, it is fly fishing–only water with restrictive creel limits. Along with the quality of the water and the abundance of insects, the state's protective management of the river is an important part of why the fishery has remained good on the Magalloway.

This stretch of the Magalloway is yet another top-notch river located below a hydroelectric dam. Wilson Mills is a long morning's worth of fishing downstream of where the river flows out of the dam on the lower end of Aziscohos Lake. Aziscohos is the larger of two lakes—the other being the even more remote Parmachenee Lake—that interrupts the Magalloway on its journey from the Canadian border down to its terminus at the edge of Lake Umbagog. Though the dam on Aziscohos is small, and the Magalloway does not feel like a tailwater, it is certainly impacted by the fact that the water levels are controlled.

We are fishing this day with guide Mike Warren. As the four of us drive from Oquossuc along Maine Route 16 around the northern side of Mooselookmeguntic and Richardson Lakes, and down the eastern side of Aziscohos to Wilson Mills, we ply our guide for information. Having worked in the area for years while running Clearwater Camps on Mooselookmeguntic Lake, Mike has a wealth of information about the region, the fishing, the ecology. But, like most Mainers, he is not effusive in his speech. Wisdom has to be pried from him. He is also ready to get out of the business and is trying to sell his beautiful camp on the lake where we have been staying this trip.

We park along the Magalloway at a public access just a few miles downstream of the Aziscohos dam. We test the water temperature. It is fifty-three degrees, warmer than I would have expected for May, but just about perfect for brook trout. There is a good hatch on. Two different species of caddis flies are on the water in decent numbers, along with mayflies known as green drakes and a large number of midges. One of the species of mayfly coming off the water looks like the *Ephemerella subvaria*, more commonly known as the Hendrickson. Maine has more than two hundred species of mayflies, more than any other state. This is particular species, though, really gets trout actively feeding. As our guide had told us, the stretch of water just below the bridge in Wilson Mills looked to be a productive spot, with a nice gravel bottom, well-aerated, good habitat for insects, and good canopy upstream. There are lots of fish in the water, and they're taking flies. The water here is easily accessible, and thus popular among fly-casters. Several other anglers are already working above and below the bridge. Fortunately, there are spots open for each of us and we are able to get out on the water as soon as we are ready.

We fish for an hour and see lots of rises, but hook only two or three fish. One consequence of fishing a popular spot, even when the vast majority of anglers practice catch-and-release, is that the fish have seen plenty of artificial flies. We speak of fish like this as being "leader shy." They are used to taking a close look at a fly before attempting to eat it. They seem to have made a connection between any sign of a leader and the possibility that the fly drifting past will not satisfy them. This makes them skittish at any hint of monofilament line. We see noses of several fish rise and take a close look at our presentations, then turn away without touching the flies.

After a while, Dave and I decide to fish our way downstream, leaving my nephew Michael with guide Mike. We are out of sight of the bridge several bends downstream when we start getting into some good trout. Two braids of the river come together with enough turbulence to have carved a deep hole in the soft river bottom. The pool looks deep enough to be over my head. Drinking deeply from its riverbank roots, a large tree lifts its branches over this hole, low and thick enough to offer good shade but high enough that I can get my line underneath.

Drifting a large double-beaded golden stonefly over the gravel, I feel the soft take of a fish just as my fly falls off the ledge of gravel at the top of the pool. I set the hook, and the soft take immediately becomes the hard pulse of a strong fish trying to shake the fly loose with thrashing tosses of its head even as it turns downstream and makes for the darkness at the bottom of the pool. This is a fish big enough to break my line if I am not careful, and the depth of the pool makes it impossible for me to follow it downstream. I feel the rush of adrenaline as I consider how to land it, and I make instinctive decisions about the amount of tension I can give to the line to turn its head. My instincts prove successful. I play the fish for a few moments. Or, rather, it plays me, until I can get in enough line. Then, reaching behind me for the net hanging on the collar of my vest, I land a sixteen-inch brookie that appears to be well-fed on the abundance of invertebrate life in this river. I hold it in the net in the current long enough to remove my hook, and then a moment longer in the water but out of the net until the fish is revived and ready to swim off on its own.

Below that corner, the river widens out and for a short stretch runs close to a dirt road. The water is more uniform here. There are no riffs or pools, no boulders or fallen logs. There is nothing to our human eyes to suggest brook trout. Still, we fish our way along, side by side, casting below a few overhanging branches where the water is deeper and perhaps some lone brookie has found a reason we have not seen to call this spot home. But we don't see any fish or even any signs of fish. We keep moving through.

Then the river bends sharply left, away from the road. After another hundred yards it enters a tight set of sharp bends and S-curves, sweeping past steep banks where the current has cut deep holes. This is classic-looking water for big brook trout. The first of several bends angle out into water that is at least armpit deep. It may be deeper. I cannot see the bottom. Sticking out from the far shore is the sort of enticing dead log with an undercutting current that every angler knows is hiding at least one trophy fish. And thus it is also the sort of log that no angler can resist. The sort of log that without a shadow of a doubt has several dozen (if not several hundred) broken-off flies hooked into it or wrapped around it. We know this because we have left our share of flies in many logs like this one, cursing them even as they drew us in as irresistibly as the call of the Sirens.

On this day, however, the loss of fly is not necessary. I work the hole with that same stonefly that enticed the previous trout to feed. I have no doubt there are fish here, so I take my time to fish it thoroughly. I work the near seam first, drifting my fly along the gravel. Along each likely line of river, I make sure to get at least one good cast, mending my line so that my fly moves naturally along the bottom. I work my casts deeper and farther across. Just on the near side of the log, a cast finally brings my fly to the attention of a waiting fish. My fly stops, and before I even have a chance to worry about the log I feel the sudden hard tug of something far more mobile than a piece of wood. I set the hook and begin another dance.

Brook trout do not often leap like rainbows and dance on their tails. They go deep and pull hard, and they do their dancing below the surface, spinning and turning and rolling in wonderfully acrobatic contortions. They also have a great knack for wrapping line around logs and branches and then breaking off. Which is to say, even without jumping, a big brookie can still put up a determined fight. And this one proves to be the sort of brook trout that many people never see in their lives because very few rivers in the Appalachians produce brook trout so big. It is a seventeen-inch squaretail with the bright red belly and underjaw of a male.

Dave joins me to admire the fish as I hold it beneath the water. When I let go, the fish moves an arm's length away but then stays there for a time, finning in the current. Finally it is gone. But I do not leave this hole. I move a few yards downstream and cast to the spot where I imagine the curve of the bottom starting to come back up, and where I also imagine another trout enjoying the safety of this deep hole, while keeping an eye on what the current might bring it. And, five minutes later, the hole produces another trout. This one is even larger and just as brightly colored as the previous two. It is a creature of unsurpassed beauty. Just to see it and hold it beneath the water for a few moments as I free it from the connection that had bound us together brings some indescribable emotion welling up in my chest and throat and eyes. Thrill. Delight. Joy. Perhaps even some sort of sorrow.

Before I leave the corner, I have landed and released three brookies be-fitting a pool that deep. While Dave looks for a fourth, I move downstream to the next corner. It doesn't look or smell or feel quite so trouty here. It is deep, but it is out of the main current and the water is sluggish, not as likely to carry a steady supply of food. The bottom is silt instead of gravel and less of a good home for the aquatic insects I associate with trout. Past this corner the river narrows and there is another nice riff and pool, and I am already eyeing that spot and considering skipping this one. Except there is a big old dead tree fallen near the bank here. It's worth at least a peek.

Sneaking along the shoreline and peering cautiously over the bank, I see the sort of brook trout I dream of. It has to be at least a four- or five-pounder. It lies below the log in the slow eddy, moving out every now and then to grab a bite of something drifting past, or swirling out of the main current into this slacker water.

Unfortunately, the pool is deep and the currents irregular and confus-ing. They seem to swirl one way up near the surface and another way down below the log. I have to work hard to get my fly to drift anywhere close to where I want it. Mathematicians and physicists call this chaos or sometimes the butterfly effect: the slightest change in where I drop my fly on the water upstream, or in how I mend my line in the current, makes a huge change in where the fly ultimately drifts along the bottom, or whether it even reaches the bottom at all. And I must also be careful not to snag on that log, and equally careful not to spook the fish with my shadow or silhouette or even with the sight of my line and artificial fly. Even on the Magalloway I might not see another fish this big for years. And so I cannot pull myself away. I make cast after cast. Some bring my fly close enough that I'm sure the fish must see it, but too far away to induce any effort on its part, or with a drift too unnatural to fool a wily trout. I make a number of other casts that are not even close. Had I not seen the fish, I would give up and move on.

But I have seen it. I still see it. It is moving in and out from the log, disappearing for a time, then appearing again. And if nothing else, I have at least been careful about my silhouette. It gives no indication that it has seen me. Or perhaps it has seen me and does not consider me a threat. Is this trout so big that the world has ceased to be a threat?

I do not give up. This fish could keep me occupied an entire morning. And finally, through an equal measure of luck and sheer repetition as much as skill and observation, I make the cast I have been working so hard to make. I find the solution to the chaos. Or else the law of probability finally works on my behalf. I land my big artificial stonefly in just the perfect place upstream and mend my line just the necessary way to get my fly to drift past the log with the somewhat natural movement a real stonefly might make if knocked lose from its gravel home upstream and sent spinning downriver. I watch the fly drifting right where I want it to. I see the trout turn toward the fly and move forward an inch or two, examining it for whatever it is a trout looks for.

It makes up its mind. Suddenly this great brook trout flashes forward and takes my fly hard. In less time than it takes me to lift my rod and set a hook, and with the skill of a finely trained surgeon making a precise cut or of a downhill racer brushing past a slalom gate at speeds more appropriate for a car, the trout turns and darts back toward its home with the fly in its mouth.

These two movements—the lifting of my rod and the return of the trout to its abode beneath the log—combine to create between us the connection of a tight fly line. It is a connection we both feel, perhaps at the exact same instant. And we both react. But while I have spent a large portion of my morning trying to make that one perfect cast with that ideal drift, this behemoth of the deep in just a few blinks of an eye succeeds in wrapping our tenuous connection around the log, breaking it off, and swimming away, leaving me standing on the bank, heart pounding, half jubilant with excitement and half devastated from loss.

I will return to the Magalloway many times in the years to come. Eventually, the stretch of water a mile or so upstream from the Wilson Mills bridge, closer to the Aziscohos dam and the generating station, will become a more favored spot. There the gradient is steeper, the water swifter, and the woods along the shore denser. It takes more work to walk the shoreline, wade the river, fish. But the anglers are more spread out there. It is usually possible to find a corner where no other casters are visible. On a May day in 2012, I am spending a day on the swifter water with Rich, another friend, who has recently retired from a college teaching career. The air is exceptionally warm for May, somewhere in the upper eighties. It is the sort of day that bespeaks of global climate change and makes the angler fear for the future of trout streams. But it's also the sort of day I accept with a certain uneasy appreciation, because the unusual afternoon heat drives off the black flies that had been brutal all morning, and all the day before. Also, the heat stimulates a late afternoon caddis hatch the likes of which I have never seen. Not anywhere. It is far denser even than the hatch that had once impressed me on the Androscoggin. It feels like a blizzard.

And yet there is no sign of trout rising to take those flies. If the brookies are taking caddis, they are doing so beneath the surface, grabbing them as they rise from the bottom to hatch. Perhaps they sense something unearthly or wrong about this hatch. Perhaps they are just not ready for it this early in the year. I try dry caddis imitations but get only a few tentative hits, and I land only one fish. I switch to a fly imitating sucker spawn, tied by Rich the evening before. I use the sucker spawn as a dropper below a big black cone-head wooly bugger. The heavy bugger is there mostly for the weight, since the sucker spawn flies are not heavy enough to get down to the bottom. But it is one more thing that will perhaps entice the trout.

The combination works better than I could hope. I catch five fat brook trout on the sucker spawn. In one ten-minute span in the early evening, when the hatch is at its thickest, I hook and land three trout in the same ten-yard stretch of river. In the midst of the blizzard of caddis, all of the fish are mysteriously ignoring the insects and instead hitting flies imitating sucker spawn, dead drifted along the bottom. There is so much going on in a river that we do not observe—at least not without work. This evening gives me just a little glimpse into that mystery.

The next day, still using my wooly bugger and sucker spawn combination, I hook a lunker in the swift current. I cannot turn it. It takes me a hundred yards downstream to the tail end of a gravel run where I can go no farther without swimming. There we must go toe-to-toe like boxers. I am patient, and my tippet holds. I net the fish in an eddy behind a big boulder. It, too, had taken the spawn pattern. I am impressed with the fishing here. I snap a photo of this fish, sitting underwater within the confines of my net, too large to lay straight. The photo will be all I bring home of this fish. Although I have caught a few brookies like this before, and expect I will do so again, this is a fish to remember.

Yet still I keep returning to that submerged log several bends below Wilson Mills where I once saw, and lost, the brook trout of my dreams. In one sense, I never again saw that behemoth of a char. Though the log is still in the same place, slowly rotting away, the fish is gone. In another sense, however, the fish is still there. I see it in my memory for the rest of the day, and for several days and weeks after that. It can still be seen there today, hiding below that log, feeding on big golden stoneflies, where it calls to my memory, "Come back."

And at those times in life when I, too, am feeling a little dead, a piece of this river stays with me like a balm, and from it there flows into me a taste of a greater resurrection power.

First Dam

Upper Dam and the Blueback Trout

Matthew Dickerson

There is something which unites magic and applied science while separating both from the "wisdom" of earlier ages. For the wise men of old the cardinal problem had been how to conform the soul to reality, and the solution had been knowledge, self-discipline, and virtue. For magic and applied science alike the problem is how to subdue reality to the wishes of men: the solution is a technique; and both, in the practice of this technique, are ready to do things hitherto regarded as disgusting and impious.

—C. S. Lewis, *The Abolition of Man*

We gather together at midday for lunch atop Upper Dam at the outlet of Maine's Mooselookmeguntic Lake, where it spills through into the North Arm of Richardson Lake. It is a bright but cold day in late May, with azure skies and only a few high wisps of clouds. A brisk breeze adds to the challenge of casting a fly.

Dave and I are here with a professional fishing guide named Mike Warren. My nephew Michael Dickerson has joined us for the week of fishing. We have been fishing all morning and our hands need a chance to warm up. The frost may have burned off before we arrived at the upper side of the dam three hours earlier, but the air had still been cold and crisp, more like late April than late May. After motoring across Mooselookmeguntic Lake, Mike had pulled his boat into a spot on the bank by the dam where the dock was supposed to be, but hadn't yet been put in for the summer. We had all climbed out carefully over a floating log used for mooring. Nobody wanted to go for a swim in that water; it would have made for a long, cold ride back across the lake.

Below Upper Dam is a big deep pool with a constant supply of turbulent, well-oxygenated water. Baitfish and insects abound. So, therefore, do the brook trout and landlocked salmon, along with an occasional lake trout. The pool narrows into a long stretch of current flowing over a nice gravelly bottom with a good mix of big boulders before it opens again into the Upper Richardson Lake. Most of the summer it is just shallow enough over that lower stretch of current that a competent wader can get out close to the middle from either side and cast, but deep enough to provide plenty of cover for big wary fish. And there is plenty of fishable water. Two anglers could spend all day here and not work all of it. There are fish by the spillways at the head of the pool, fish at the tail of the pool, fish in the shallower channel along both sides, and even fish along the wooded southern shore where fewer anglers bother to cast. When the water is low enough, I like to wade out to one of the big boulders. I can cast contentedly from the same boulder for an hour and not feel like I've worked all the water within reach.

It had not been a bad morning of fishing, though certainly not as good as our last trip here on a June day the previous year, with Dave's son Michael. We've been landing perhaps a fish an hour. Still, though the fishing has been slower than expected, we are excited to be here. When it comes to brook trout, we are standing on holy ground. We are a short distance away from the site of the cabin where, in 1924, the legendary flytier Carrie Stevens, wife of a Maine fishing guide named Wallace Stevens, created the now famous streamer fly known as the grey ghost. Tied with a feather that provides a natural eye pattern, the grey ghost is a deadly imitation of the smelt and other small baitfish that inhabit many of Maine's best lakes. Carrie tied hers, as she tied all her flies, without the aid of a vise, holding the hook in one hand and wrapping with the other. She did not herself often fish, but rather spent her time tying flies for others. After creating the grey ghost, however, she decided to try out her own fly in the pool below the dam. She landed a brook trout just short of seven pounds. Her reputation as a flytier was established.

And rightly so. For many years, I have used the grey ghost along with many other variations of streamers modeled after that first simple pattern. Though I have not (yet) caught a six-pound brookie, I've felt the thrill of many one- to three-pounders slamming my line, chasing flies based on Carrie's. I have removed grey ghosts from the jaws of brook trout that have been gorging on smelt. As I remove my smelt imitation, I will see three or four of the real things sticking out the sides of the trout's mouth. I've done this since well before I ever heard the name Stevens, or had thought of visiting Upper Dam.

But it is not just the sites where Carrie tied—and then successfully tried—her famous fly that are holy, magical, and romantic. It is the entire area. The bodies of water in the Rangeley Lakes region of Maine, especially Mooselookmeguntic, were famous in the nineteenth century not only for their natural beauty but also for their world-class brook trout, which routinely grew to be six to ten pounds. When word spread about the quality of this famous brook trout fishery, there was a hatch of hotels and fishing camps on the lakes, and rail spurs were built so that presidents and senators and other wealthy and powerful fishermen could get here. The walls of these camps have faded photos of poles laden with huge trout, held up by two men.

This substantial set of large natural lakes, up to seventeen miles long and several miles wide—lakes with Algonquian names like Mooselookmeguntic (which means "moose feeding place"), Cupsuptic ("closed-up stream"), Umbagog ("clear lake"), Kennebago ("long pond"), Aziscohos ("small pine trees"), and Parmachenee (named after an Abenaki chieftain's daughter), as well as English names like Rangeley and Richardson—sit between two spur lines of the Appalachians with Old Blue and Elephant Mountains on one side, and Mount Pisgah and Black Mountain on the other. The lowest of the lakes, Umbagog, is 1,245 feet above sea level. Little Kennebago Lake, about thirty miles away by car, sits much higher up at 1,772 feet.

These are high elevations for natural lakes above the 45th parallel (closer to the North Pole than the equator), and so close to the ocean (barely a hundred miles from the Atlantic, as the crow files), and as large as they are (Mooselookmeguntic is over twenty-five square miles in area, and closer to thirty counting its northern arm, Cupsuptic Lake). And the group of large ponds at the very top of Kennebago River are even higher, up around two thousand feet.

These are mountain lakes. Appalachian lakes. And they are also re-mote. With the exception of Rangeley Lake, which is girdled by a state road and has been developed, the rest of these massive lakes with their dozens of miles of shoreline have at most one short stretch of a hundred yards where they are accessible by public road with one public boat landing. All other access is by boat, or by plane, or by rough gravel road—usually a private logging road. The private road to Upper Dam is doubly gated, making the dam accessible only by a half-mile hike prior to June and a much longer hike later in the summer. It is, as they say, in the middle of nowhere.

And that, in a very roundabout way, brings us back to Upper Dam where we are fly fishing. The dam sits on the outlet of Mooselookmegun-tic Lake in the middle of all this incredible water, connecting the cold high tributaries to the Androscoggin River that will eventually carry this water to the Atlantic Ocean. Sitting on the dam, we thought again about the history of these lakes, and their famous brook trout fishing in the late nineteenth century. We thought about famous public figures who came by rail to visit and fish these famous waters for their eight-pound trout—rail that is supposed to race us away from the industrialized city to the pristine wilderness shoreline, yet that often succeeds not as an escape from indus-trialization but merely as an extension of it. When it came to brook trout, of all the lakes in the region the best was Mooselookmeguntic. Living in this lake was a rare species of char, a cousin of the brook trout called the blueback trout or *S. oquassa* (or *S. alpinus oquassa*), which is closely related to the Sunapee trout (*S. aureolus*) that once lived in scattered ponds in New Hampshire and in my home state of Vermont. Though they could grow bigger, blueback trout were usually only about five or six inches long, and lived most of their lives in the deepest, coldest waters of the lake. But for a couple of weeks each year they would come out of the depths and spawn up the tributaries around the Maine fishing town of Oquossuc. They were so abundant that some reports indicate residents of Oquossuc would net them and use them as garden fertilizer. Their brook trout cousins grew to their enormous sizes by feasting on the abundant little bluebacks. The blueback trout, it seemed, were a vital factor in the trophy brook trout fishing.

In 1880, a fish and game club in Oquossuc decided that it could also engineer some better fishing by introducing into Mooselookmeguntic some landlocked salmon, which were widely distributed in other Maine lakes. Landlocked salmon (*Salmo salar*) is the same species as the famed Atlantic salmon, one of the world's most prized coldwater game fish, and one closely related to the European brown trout (*S. trutta*). The retreating of glaciers and blockage of rivers many centuries ago trapped some of these magnificent anadromous fish in newly created lakes where they adapted to permanent freshwater life. Though they don't grow as large in lakes as in the Atlantic Ocean, they remain a wonderful fighting fish, every bit as acrobatic as the rainbow trout. It is Maine's official state fish. When I first started going to Rapid River, it was as much or more for the incredible thrill of landing a four- or five-pound landlocked salmon in a class III rapid as it was for the brook trout. But *S. salar* were not native to Mooselookmeguntic. And so the fish and game club, whose members also thrilled at catching these wonderful fish, introduced them to Mooselookmeguntic Lake.

Within about thirty years, the blueback trout were extinct in the lake.

It would be naïve to claim that the extinction of the blueback trout was entirely or even primarily the result of the introduction of landlocked salmon into their lake. Life is rarely that simple. The fact that the people of Oquossuc had used bluebacks as fertilizer probably didn't help the rare little char. But their disappearance may have been influenced by the introduction of landlocked salmon, which unlike the brook trout (or in combination with brook trout) were able to consume the bluebacks to the point of extinction. With the bluebacks gone, the brook trout had lost an important source of food. Brook trout are voracious predators. Living in streams and rivers, and eating a diet of insects, they may grow to fifteen or sixteen inches. At some point, though, to become real behemoths, they need to start eating other fish. With blueback trout gone, by the early twentieth century the trophy-sized brook trout slowly disappeared and eventually ceased to be found in Mooselookmeguntic Lake. The introduction of salmon may have helped improve the famous fishing in one way, but in another way it also helped destroy it.

Chapter 2

Brook Trout in New York and Pennsylvania

Learning the Rhythms of the River

David O'Hara

In our family, there was no clear line between religion and fly fishing. We lived at the junction of great trout rivers in western Montana, and our father was a Presbyterian minister and a fly fisherman who tied his own flies and taught others. He told us about Christ's disciples being fishermen, and we were left to assume, as my brother and I did, that all first-class fishermen on the Sea of Galilee were fly fishermen and that John, the favorite, was a dry-fly fisherman.

—Norman Maclean, *A River Runs Through It*

LOADING THE LINE

The boundary between the woods and the river where we are walking is not clearly defined. The river runs under the woods—or perhaps the woods grow into the river. At any rate, as much as we might wish to distinguish between them, the woods and the river resist such distinctions. At some points near where they meet one is not sure whether one is in the woods or the river or both. Between the roots of trees are sinkholes full of river water, and you can see the water flowing though those holes even before you emerge from the woods into the river. By the time you push aside the last layers of heavy underbrush to view the open river, you're already shin-deep in cold, clear water.

My son Michael and I push back those last branches and then stand there and look at the open river. It's wide and fast, and not a little unnerving. In front of us, maybe twenty yards out and a hundred yards below the century-old dam, the top of a boulder peeks out of the river. The water is clear, and we can see the bottom just fine, so we step toward the boulder. The water is clear, but deceptive. It is now up above our knees. Another step, and it's above my waist. Michael is shorter than I am, and looks at me a little apprehensively. I step farther. It's up to my rib cage, and I'm standing on top of a submerged rock. If my foot slips, I'll be in even deeper water. I strap my rod to my vest so my hands are free, and I unfold my wading staff. Holding the staff in one hand, I reach back to Michael with my other hand. Thus connected by a tight handclasp, together we tiptoe, probing with the steel tip of the wading staff for purchase underwater, each of us giving balance to the other as we slip and leap in six feet of water from one submerged boulder to another. Finally, we reach the big rock and clamber on top, relieved. For now we will not think of the trip back to shore. Once I am standing, I look at the river on the other side of the boulder. I cannot see the bottom. It must be twenty feet deep or more.

I tie on a smelt imitation, a streamer I tied myself. Casting with a fly rod is not easy to learn, and Michael is still a novice at it, so I cast the streamer for him so he can fish. With my five-weight rod I whip out a few yards of floating line then switch to a double-haul, a difficult cast. But it's the cast I need if I'm going to get the fly into the wind and upstream where I know the fish are. The line curls forward, straightens out, then shoots back over me again, parallel yellow lines in the air. I am not throwing the hook, which is too light to cast; I am throwing the weight of the line. As it reaches its full extension, I wait for it to "load," then haul it back through the guides with my left hand while my right arm brings the rod forward again. I repeat this action, each time letting more line out from the reel. Timing is everything, waiting for the line to load or straighten out, feeling it load and then responding to it in order to speed it up again.

I don't look at the line. I don't know when I stopped looking at the line, but it has become unnecessary for me to do so now, and if I do look, I'm sure to mess myself up and tie a "wind knot." I wait for it, and finally there is enough line in the air in front of me, and I release the tension, laying my rod down. The line floats to the water silently, and the tiny smelt lands gently on the surface. This is the rhythm I want my son to learn, even as I am still, after many years, continuing to learn it myself.

I hand the rod to Michael. Holding the rod in his right hand, he strips the line in rhythmically, as I have taught him. He tugs the line down and to the left with his left hand. Tug, then wait. Tug, then wait. The smelt surges a few feet, pauses, surges again. Tug, then wait. We both feel the tension of the moment as the smelt streamer pulses like a heartbeat. We cannot see the drama underwater, but we know that more than one fish is eyeing the smelt; upstream we have seen them break the surface, chasing other smelt. Tug, then wait. Tug, bang! A thousand droplets of water spring like mist from the suddenly taut line. The rod bows down toward the dam. Michael lifts the rod to set the hook and the rod bends nearly double.

For a moment his life and the brook trout's are connected, and it is not clear what is the boundary between the two. The line vibrates with the vitality of each of them. The philosopher Michael Polanyi tells us that when we use a tool, we may distinguish between two types of attention we pay. He writes,

> When we use a hammer to drive in a nail, we attend to both nail and hammer, but in a different way. We watch the effect of our strokes on the nail and try to wield the hammer so as to hit the nail most effectively. When we bring down the hammer we do not feel that its handle has struck our palm but that its head has struck the nail. Yet in a sense we are certainly alert to the feelings in our palm and the fingers that hold the hammer. They guide us in handling it effectively, and the degree of attention that we give to the nail is given to the same extent but in a different way to these feelings. The difference may be stated by saying that the latter are not, like the nail, objects of our attention, but instruments of it. They are not watched in themselves; we watch something else while keeping intensely aware of them. I have a subsidiary awareness of the feeling in the palm of my hand which is merged into my focal awareness of my driving in the nail.[3]

Polanyi goes on to say that

> Our subsidiary awareness of tools and probes can be regarded now as the act of making them form a part of our own body. The way we use a hammer or a blind man uses his stick, shows in fact that in both cases we shift outwards the points at which we make contact

with the things that we observe as objects outside ourselves. While we rely on a tool or a probe, these are not handled as external objects. . . . We pour ourselves out into them and assimilate them as parts of our own existence. We accept them existentially by dwelling in them.[4]

To put it differently, as we become more familiar with a tool, that tool becomes an extension of our knowing selves. Novices use tools; masters dwell in them. The old saying about "the right tool for the right job" suggests that the place of tools is to acquaint ourselves with different parts of the world. Learning to use tools opens us up to experiences that would otherwise remain over the horizon of possibility for us. We don't often think of fishing rods as tools, but in this sense, that's exactly what they are. They are a way of knowing the world, a way of making contact with a part of the world that would otherwise remain unknown to us.

As Michael learns to hold the rod and play the fish, the rod is becoming an extension of Michael's knowing self. So is the line becoming an extension of Michael. And here is the curious thing, the mystery every fisher is at least vaguely aware of: the line is connected to the fish. Where does the tool end, where does the experienced world begin? The fisherman knows the trout as no one else knows it; the fisherman and the trout are vitally connected.

Now Michael pulls the line in more deliberately, urging the fish toward our rock. The fish wants to go anywhere but where it is pulled, so he must bring it without pulling it. His tippet is 7x, only a pound and a half in tensile strength. This fish weighs at least that much, and is capable of pulling much harder if it gets the strength of the river behind it. Michael must persuade the fish to come near so that we may release it. If he muscles it in, the line will break. If he lets the line go slack, the fish will spit the hook. He must let his arms feel every motion of the fish and respond in a way that will draw the fish where it least wants to go and most needs to go. Michael learns quickly, and soon he has it up to the edge of the rock. It's a fat nineteen-inch brook trout, *Salvelinus fontinalis*. It is a beautiful fish, with its green vermiculated back shading gently to gold-and-red-freckled sides and a pale belly. It has every color from dark green to bright red, and its fins have vivid white stripes at their leading edges. It looks like the river, like it has been touched by some prince of painters. It is like the ring-necked pheasant rooster, vividly colored and camouflaged all at once, a spare but regal beauty.

I am not the first to notice the beauty of this fish. The Iroquois neighbors of my Algonquin ancestors in New York have admired it for thousands of years, if Nick Karas is right. In his book *Brook Trout*, he recounts this story:

> According to Indian Legend, brook trout were not always the speckled beauties we know today. "Once, long ago," said old Jesse Logan, of the Cornplanter Reservation in Warren County, Pennsylvania, the last (in 1928) of the Shikellemus tribe, "when Manitou visited the land of the Iroquois to lead His lost children back to the Happy Hunting Ground in the Far East, He grew weak with hunger and cold on his long quest. Toward night He stopped beside a pool in the Seneca country [New York] which was overshadowed by colossal white pines and hemlocks. Noticing that it was full of handsome trout, as black as ebony, He reached in His hand and easily caught the largest of the superb fish. Looking at it He was struck by its beauty and agile grace, and decided to control His hunger and let it live, so He dropped it back into the deep pool.
>
> The trout went its way, but instantly its sides took on a silvery hue where the fingers of the Great Spirit had held it, and all of its kind became marked with the same silvery sheen and many colored spots and halos, as a token of their having been handled by the kindly Manitou. For that reason, the Seneca Indians and others of the Six Nations would not eat brook trout. Brook trout were sacred to the highest instincts of their race. But what the redmen spared," said Logan, "white men destroyed by the millions."[5]

Unlike Manitou, Michael and I do not even remove the fish from the water or touch it with our hands. Michael dips the rod, its tip lowering quickly enough to let the trout spit the barbless hook with a single breath of water. For a moment, hovering in the current, eyeing us, the fish is still. I give silent thanks as we release this first brookie of the day. It is tempting to hold it out of the water for a photograph, but every moment out of the water brings greater likelihood that the fish will not survive this encounter. If we release it gently, it is very unlikely to die. It is beautiful now, but if we were to keep it, its bright colors would fade even before we got it home to cook it. What Manitou's hand has done, ours can easily undo if we are careless. Over the years I have come to practice a kind of first-fruits offering, giving back to the river the first fish I catch—which, for some reason, is very hard to do—and I want to teach Michael to do the same. The brookie turns gently and swims away.

Michael does not spend much time outdoors, and I was a little anxious about bringing him on this trip. We've spent several nights in a tent, bitten by too many bugs of too many kinds. He is worn out. But just after he releases the fish, he looks at me and says, "I think I like fly fishing!" He is beaming. I have not seen him smile much since we started camping. Inside, I am beaming too.

AT HOME IN THE CATSKILLS

I grew up in the Catskill Mountains of New York, a subset of the Appalachians that form the western side of the Hudson Valley. The mountains are round, ancient hills rising a few thousand feet above sea level. They once towered like the Rockies, but they are much older and, like the whole Appalachian chain, bowed down and smoothed over by weather and age. The Catskills are covered with unbroken forest except for those places, maybe a thousand feet above the valley floor, where the glaciers slowly marked them as their own, leaving cliffs hundreds of feet high.

In those mountains I am never lost, because I can always look up and spot a familiar peak and find my way home using it as a beacon. And if the tree canopy is too thick to find a peak, water will always lead me home. When I was a child, my father taught me that if I ever got lost in the woods, I only needed to walk downhill until I found a stream, then follow that stream until I came to people. All the towns and cities of the Catskills have water flowing through them, and you can never go far before you find another stream that flows into one of those towns.

Like many Americans, I've got a little bit of native blood, just a little, and that Mohican heritage has always meant a lot to my father, in part because it meant a lot to his Uncle Charlie, who taught him woodcraft. Because it matters to him, it matters to me. Dad walks carefully and consciously in the woods, listening to them and letting them show him what they hold. He's an engineer by training, but nothing seems to fill him with wonder as the forest does. Dad can walk as silently as a cat in the woods, and he can vanish from sight in an instant. Dad has made me feel at home in these woods, reminding me that they have been our family home for thousands of years. As a child I would walk the fine ruts of deer trails in the hillside behind my home, following them to the chains of ponds and swamps that formed my favorite playgrounds, and I would imagine my ancestors ten or twenty generations ago doing the same.

RECESS

Many of the streams of my childhood have no names except the names of the streams they flow into. When, as a child, I wanted to fish, I had only to pick a direction and walk. No matter which way I went, I'd find a stream within a mile or less, and all the streams around me held brook trout.

Twenty-five centuries ago Xenophon wrote that if a young man wanted an education, he should learn to hunt. Xenophon added that if the boy had money left over after that, he should buy some books and go to school, too. If Xenophon had lived in the Catskills, he might have said that a boy should learn to fish. The streams of the Catskills aren't just playgrounds, they are a university, and class is always in session.[6] A small, unnamed trout stream divided our elementary school's parking lot from its playground, and another, the Sawkill Creek, ran through the woods along its eastern edge.

One day, in sixth grade, Boey Koeppen and I waited for the playground monitors to look away and then we darted into the woods and made a bee-line for the Sawkill. The Sawkill is a small river, maybe sixty or seventy feet wide, with alternating deep riffles and chest-deep pools of clear water flowing over smooth stones. It's full of trout, suckers, and sculpins, turtles, snakes, salamanders, and frogs, and abundant invertebrate life dwells under its stones on the bottom.

We lay on our bellies on large flat rocks at the edge of the stream, our faces hovering over the water, and turned over the smaller stones in the pool in front of us, searching for crayfish. Soon the monitors blew their whistle to call us all in for class again. We heard it and ignored it. Something told us that the lessons of this stream were far better than any lessons we'd have indoors. As it turns out, Mr. Van Bramer did not entirely agree with this assessment of the educational value of his lesson plans.

After an hour or so of catching crayfish and frogs and inspecting the local copperhead snake population, Boey and I decided we should probably rejoin the class. When we walked into the classroom we made a brief showing of ignorance and muttered something about not realizing recess had ended, but our hearts weren't in it.

Mr. Van Bramer obviously felt obligated to chew us out, and he had plainly been concerned about us. He picked up the classroom phone and called the principal to let him know that we had been found and they could call off the search. I swallowed hard, and stole a glance at Boey. It hadn't occurred to us that anyone would notice we were missing, or that they'd be worried about us being lost. After all, we never felt lost when we were by a stream. Mr. Van Bramer didn't tolerate foolishness and he was known for running a tight ship. We stood like soldiers in front of the class and prepared ourselves for the worst, but it never came. All we got was a lecture—albeit a stern one—about staying away from the Sawkill and making sure adults knew where we were. As he rebuked us in front of the class, I watched his eyes, the windows of his soul. The rest of his face was trying to mete out judgment, but his eyes were all sympathy. It was plain to both of us even then that he was not so much angry as envious, and maybe even a little proud of us.

Mr. Van Bramer was a world traveler, and every month or so he'd show us slides of one of the places he had visited. I still remember seeing his slide of the Tío Pepe sign in the Puerta del Sol in Madrid, and thinking, "I want to go there." Years later I lived in Madrid, not too far from that sign, and I often silently thank Mr. Van Bramer for showing me those slides. He showed them not to boast but to provoke us, as he did when he occasionally spoke to us in German, as a way of saying, "Look. The world is bigger than you know. And you've got to go see it. Don't waste your lives." I went back to visit him once, when I was in high school, to thank him. I gave him a coin I got on one of my travels—I think it was from India—as a token of gratitude for the example he set. Every time I travel I think of him, and I wonder where his latest travels have taken him.

A few months after Boey and I skipped class, Mr. Van Bramer himself took us all down to the stream and had us turn over rocks to see what was under them. "What are we looking for?" we asked. "Just look," he said, "and let's see what's there." When I turned over my first rock, a leggy little freshwater isopod darted away from me, maybe an inch and a half long. I caught it in a cup and showed it to Boey. It was the first isopod I'd ever seen, and it was magical. Not that isopods themselves are magical, but seeing something new can be. Boey and I had spent a lot of time looking under rocks, and we thought we knew what was under them. It turns out that we only knew how to find what we were already looking for. Mr. Van Bramer gave me the gift of seeing something I didn't even know was there. Years later I learned to see the larval mayflies and stoneflies that cling to the rocks, and the many other invertebrates like caddisflies in the cases they make, and long, eerie hellgrammites. More importantly, I'm aware that I'm still not seeing all the life that clings to the rocks. More than once I've stared at a rock, thinking I've seen it all, then something I've never seen before starts to move right under my eyes. One moment it looks like leaf litter or algae; the next moment it's an arthropod. Just because light reflects off something and hits our retinas doesn't mean we've seen it.

Occasionally I teach a reef ecology course on a barrier island in Belize. Those early lessons on the Sawkill come in handy there as my students and I walk in tidal pools and turn over rocks together. As we hold the brown pieces of coral in our hands, at first they appear to be covered with nothing more than multihued algae. If we look patiently and let our eyes adjust from what we expect to see to what the coral wants to show us, brilliant nudibranchs begin to appear, slowly slipping across the coral at a smooth gelatinous pace. Tiny transparent shrimp appear like miniature masterpieces from some glassblower's workshop, only their eyes and internal organs visible. A decorator crab will begin to shift uncomfortably in the sunlight, and at first it looks like a bit of algae moving on its own. The crab might be smaller than my thumbnail, its legs like green toothpicks. Like some freshwater caddisflies, the decorator crab picks up bits of its environment and fashions camouflage for itself, its carapace a rooftop garden of its own making. Each piece of coral is a whole world, encrusted with layer upon layer of ingenious life. Chitons, fireworms, and barnacles appear, and infinitesimal brittle stars try to edge further into some crevice. Porifera and new coral growth alive with zooxanthellae dapple the dead coral head with fresh color. Every species finds its niche, and the longer we look the more we see.

This is more than entertainment. My colleague Craig Spencer and I bring our students to Belize because we both grew up around water and we know that what we teach them in the classroom will fade in time, but they will never forget what the water teaches their hands and eyes.

We bring them to these waters for another reason as well: these vital places are also fragile places, and what happens in streams and mangroves and reefs can be an indicator of what will soon happen farther down the ecological stream. The invertebrates in a mountain stream can be extremely sensitive to changes in water chemistry. A shift in the pH or in saturated minerals, the introduction of toxins from urban or agricultural runoff, or a change in water temperature can produce a dramatic change in the invertebrate life in a stream. So monitoring the invertebrates can be a way to keep an eye on the health of the watershed.

I haven't seen Mr. Van Bramer since I was in high school, and I lost touch with Boey twenty years ago. Last time I saw him we were fishing the same spot on the Sawkill, a half mile down from the elementary school, and pulling in a lot of fine trout. Then I went off to college in Vermont and he joined the air force and became crew chief for a refueling tanker based in South Dakota. Then, in an odd twist, I moved to South Dakota for a job and he left the service and moved back to the Northeast. I ran into him again not too long ago, after his father and my mother had died. He goes by Bo now, no longer Boey. He's lean and muscular, and his face is worn by sun and wind. His hands, trained in fixing anything from small engines to fighter jets, are strong and callused. We fall to talking about the Sawkill, which runs through his backyard and sometimes, in bad years, floods his basement. Sometime soon, we say, we should fish it together.

SPECKLED TROUT

The Catskills are famous for brook trout, and there are some famous streams in the Hudson Valley, like the Battenkill. I admit I've never been interested in fishing the famous streams, because the ones near home—streams like the Sawkill, the upper Esopus, and especially their many tiny tributaries— were so good, and so interesting. I have a feeling some local decided to write a story about how good the Battenkill was in order to make sure that angling tourists went to fish there rather than to the really good streams of the Catskills. The "-kill" in Catskill and Battenkill comes from an old Dutch word meaning "stream." (A few years ago PETA petitioned to change the name of the Fishkill because they thought it suggested cruelty, when in fact it just means "fish creek.") The Catskill Mountains are filled with cold, clear kills, or streams, that course freely yearlong through steep cloves and high waterfalls down to slower freestone streams, finally wending their way across silted bottoms to empty into the Hudson River. The Catskills provide much of the water for New York City's eight million people, stored in deep reservoirs like the Ashokan, a few miles from my boyhood home. Further north from my home in Woodstock, near Palenville, is the Kaaterskill Creek that falls through the Kaaterskill Clove, a long series of waterfalls and plunge pools full of trout and a great place to test youthful bravado for those willing to leap from cliffs into the cold water twenty or thirty feet below. These can be hard places to fish, and angling here is part rock climbing, part precision casting. But the hard places to fish are often the best places. In places like this, you don't just catch fish, you achieve them.

Now that I no longer live in New York, I find I long to return to fish in New York. When I get the chance, I do go back, and I always fish familiar streams, like the Sawkill and its tributaries, to reacquaint myself with the waters of my youth. The Sawkill has its headwaters near Overlook Mountain, and it tumbles down through towns and reservoirs and deep forests for several dozen miles on its way to the Hudson. In years of fishing it, I still have not walked its whole length. These are the waters my father taught me to love when, on the first of April, we would pack lunches and head out early for opening day of trout season. We rarely caught anything, but the streams were full of wonder and delight. We'd walk along the banks and throw rocks, look at debris from recent floods, admire beaver dams and the power of water to undercut banks. We'd stand on slippery rocks at the foot of a waterfall and crane our necks back to gaze up at the falling water and shout to each other over the sound of it crashing on the rocks below. Or we'd stand on bridges and gaze down at the sleek shapes finning in the slow places downstream of rocks and darting into the current to seize food as it passed. My father didn't try to teach me much on those trips, but I learned a lot from walking along the banks, chatting with him, and coming to see what he saw. He looked at the banks with his engineer's eye and showed me how rivers are always remaking themselves and cutting new channels, how something as soft as water could cut something as hard as rock with thunderous elegance and glacial patience.

TEACHING MY SONS TO FISH

Now I am a father, and it is my turn to walk in streams with my sons. Flash forward twenty years, and you find me standing in a small stream with Michael, on his first fishing trip with me. He is nine years old, and he is learning to fish. We are living in central Pennsylvania, and we've driven a few miles into the mountains southeast of State College. Some people who fish jokingly say, "I'd tell you the name of that stream, but then I'd have to kill you." (At least, I think they're joking.) Anyway, I'd tell you the name of this stream, but like so many of the creeks of my youth, I don't think it has one. This tiny stream reminds me of the streams I grew up with in New York, its bottom covered with smooth, round stones and its banks lined with thorny blackberries and tall goldenrod. We've parked the car a few hundred yards downstream and walked along the boulders of the stream to a deep plunge pool. I fished here a week ago and found it to be another place of wonder.

Last week, when I hiked further upstream, I nearly stepped on a fawn that was trying to hide from me by huddling under a fallen log. As I stepped over the log, it burst out and ran off into thick cover, leaving me with my heart pounding with fear and thrill. A little later a bold brown mink darted across the stream in front of me, and further still a turkey flew away into the trees. But most exciting for me was a monstrous brook trout, probably eighteen inches long and weighing several pounds, living in a thick tangle of logs.

It's too far to hike with Michael to that spot, but I bet there are trout here in this plunge pool. We approach it carefully, and I whisper to him, "Go ahead. They're in there." He casts to the far side of the pool and reels in his little Mepps spinner. Only a moment after it hits the water, the fish hits the Mepps, and Michael's first cast brings in a ten-inch brown trout. Once again, our hearts are pounding. We put the fish in our creel to bring it home for tonight's dinner, and he casts again. Halfway across the pool a rainbow trout even bigger than the brown crashes into his spinner. He's got it hooked, and he plays it well. Soon it is in the creel. We don't need words, and it's hard to find them anyway. "Nice job!" I say, but I mean much more than that. He smiles. "Wow," he says. I understand; he means a lot more, too.

A week later I crimp down the barb on a bait hook and slide it through a nightcrawler I dug out of my vegetable garden. When I fish, it's almost always with a fly rod, but I don't want my kids to get frustrated with learning to cast a fly when they're so young. So few people learn to fish anymore, I want to make sure to introduce them to this world as young as I can, so I'm willing to use bait and other lures when I fish with the kids.

I hand the rod to my other son, Matthew, who is just five years old. We're standing on the banks of Whipple Dam, where a small trout stream has been impounded to make a recreation area. The water behind the dam is not deep, and the sun warms it up like a bathtub in August. Good for swimming, but not good for trout. As water warms, it holds less saturated oxygen, and fast-moving trout need a lot of oxygen. The air you and I breathe is about 20 percent oxygen, but very cold water holds something like fifteen parts per million of oxygen, or a bit more than a thousandth of one percent. In other words, there's about 20,000 times more oxygen in air than in cold water. Warmer water might hold only half that amount of oxygen.

There are stocked brook trout in Whipple Dam, and I don't feel bad about harvesting some for dinner, since they won't last long in this heat anyway. Matthew casts the worm, and we wait. It isn't long before his bobber moves in a tap, tap, tap motion. "Lift the rod," I tell him, and he sets the hook perfectly. He hauls in a foot-long brookie. Even though it is paler than its wild-born cousins, this hatchery fish still shows the fingerprints of Manitou. It is a beautiful fish, a gift.

ACID WASH

This part of the country has some top-quality trout fishing. I imagine that anyone who is lucky enough to fish Spruce Creek will know what I mean. Spruce Creek boasts miles of beautiful spring creek fishery, with good room for casting and deep, cool water that holds lots of beautiful trout. Or so I am told, anyway. I've never fished it, because more or less the entire riverbank on both sides is privately owned, and you can't fish it unless you know someone who will let you have access. I could pay a guide who has access, I suppose. I don't mind paying guides to teach me about new water, but something rankles when I think about paying for the privilege of getting wet, in a place I won't be able to visit again until I pay again. Besides, there's excellent fishing to be had on waters with good public access in this part of the state.

This idea of access to water and of water rights is a curious and contentious one. Laws about water access vary across the country. In the New England states, both law and practice tend to treat water as common property, to which all citizens have a right of access and use. There are exceptions, of course, but in general rivers big enough to float a canoe on are fairly easy to access in New England. A few western states, like Oregon and Montana, maintain similar ideas. But in general, the farther west you go from New England, the more restrictive those laws and practices become. In some states, if a landowner owns both banks, she owns the river bottom as well, and has the right to prohibit even the dropping of an anchor from a drift boat. Pennsylvania has fairly liberal laws about access, but in practice, the trout streams of central Pennsylvania are fiercely guarded by those who own the banks. I tend to fish the Little Juniata, just downstream of where Spruce Creek flows into it, because there I can get into the water. I also am in the habit of walking long distances in streams. If I can get in the stream at a public access, I'm willing to stay in the stream for miles in order to get to the good fishing, and to defend my right to stay in the stream to anyone who challenges me.

The rivers in central Pennsylvania, like the roads, run with the mountains, and the mountains are folded in continuous pleats across the middle of the state, slow waves of rock splashing tectonically against rock, ripples under the forest. The mountains aren't peaks but long ridges running for unbroken miles, from the Delaware River down to Maryland. Look at the roads on a modern map and you will see where the valleys are, and you can imagine the ridges between them. In the valley bottoms flow larger streams, like Bald Eagle Creek and the Little Juniata, and down the ridges flow hundreds of tiny streams that feed them. Those tiny streams are, or were once, the nurseries of brook trout. Unlike the roads and the rivers, the streams tend to flow perpendicular to the mountains, straight down the mountainsides, branching out from the rivers at the valley bottoms like the veins on an alder leaf. Building a few miles of new road in central Pennsylvania might mean having to cross dozens of these little streams. A few years ago they finished Interstate Highway 99, making a much better and safer road between State College and Altoona. In order to avoid all the small towns and farms in the valley, I-99 was carved into the side of Bald Eagle Mountain, above Bald Eagle Creek. Trees and topsoil were scraped aside, and rock dynamited and trucked away, exposing the acidic bones of the mountain. Now every stream that I-99 crosses—that is, every stream on that side of Bald Eagle Creek—has had its pH drop, sometimes quite dramatically.

Some of the rivers of central Pennsylvania have natural buffers built into them that keep the water chemistry fairly stable. These so-called chalk streams flow over deposits of calcium carbonate or other minerals that leach carbonate and bicarbonate ions into the water. These streams are much more resistant to acidification, whether from mining, road construction, or acid rain. Some of the chalk streams of central Pennsylvania are rich with invertebrate life, much of it living in thick weedbeds on chalky bottoms, challenging and very rewarding places to fish with nymphs.

The bugs in these chalk rivers are remarkably diverse. The mayfly hatches can be simply majestic, as the names of the mayflies suggest: Green Drakes, Sulphurs, Blue-Winged Olives, and March Browns often abound during the summer hatches, some of the best I've seen anywhere. Caddisflies and many other aquatic insects can be found in great numbers, too.

Once I took the kids to a bug fair put on by Penn State's entomology department. In plastic shoeboxes one student displayed several long hellgrammites she had somehow caught in the bottom of one of the rivers I regularly waded in. Hellgrammites look like enormous centipedes with great mandibles for catching small fish. The hellgrammites swung their heads around the shoeboxes, looking for food, or an exit, or revenge. I was torn between fascination and a desire to flee these benthic monsters.

All this invertebrate life can be a helpful sign of the health of a stream, but it is not immediately obvious whether a stream is clean or not. Some invertebrates, like leeches, midge fly larvae, and snails, are very resistant to environmental changes. Others, like stoneflies, mayflies, and caddisflies, are very sensitive. And, of course, there are lots of ways in which a stream can be unhealthy. Spring Creek is an incredibly beautiful stream that flows through State College. It, too, has a fairly rich aquatic insect ecology, and it produces some enormous trout. Sometimes the kids and I would go downstream to Bellefonte, where fishing is not permitted, to feed the pods of huge trout swimming in the current in the center of town. Upstream, between Bellefonte and State College, I have often seen trout so large that at first I thought they were small beavers or muskrats, as they shot out from the cover of a submerged log to seize some hapless passing caddisfly. I asked a friend who is an oncologist and also a fly fisherman whether he ever keeps any fish from Spring Creek. "Oh, you can eat the fish from Spring Creek," he says, with a wry grin, "but if you do, you'll die." Spring Creek is lovely to look at, but it has a toxic history. It was slowly poisoned years ago through farm and wastewater runoff, and through discharges from various industries located along its banks. In 1956 sodium cyanide was poured down the drain at the Naval Ordnance Research Lab at Penn State, killing nearly everything in the river for miles downstream, including some 140,000 trout in one hatchery, and surely tens of thousands of trout in the river. That single spill, beginning in a drain inside a building, was toxic for sixteen miles or more downstream. While the river appears to have recovered from that spill, I'm told that the Green Drake mayfly hasn't been seen on the river since. In the 1960s and 1970s, several other highly toxic spills originated from the Nease Chemical Company. Today, if you dip a fine mesh net in the gravel along its bank you'll find a rich sampling of trout food. Many insects have recovered from the toxic spills, but it is harder to recover from a steady source of acidity. Chalk streams like Spruce Creek, Big Spring Creek, and a number of other small creeks in the region have a good deal of limestone buffering built into them, so the trout and the insects they live on are thriving.

Unfortunately, the streams that flow down Bald Eagle Mountain are not chalk streams, so the mineral runoff from the I-99 cut was like dumping acid into their veins; its effects were swift and deadly. The fish and wildlife service and state engineers have tried to buffer those streams with bags of crushed limestone, but their efforts may be too little, too late. The limestone attempts to make those streams into chalk streams, but this only works if there is enough chalk for all the water to flow through, and if there is time for the chalk to dissolve in the water. And if it is done high enough upstream. If you put in the chalk bags too high, then water that trickles in below won't be buffered. But if you put it in too low, you are in effect cutting off the upper reaches of a stream to fish migration and to insect life. Many aquatic insects live most of their lives underwater but then, at the moment of sexual maturity, undergo a metamorphosis and fly to mate and deposit their eggs, often in a different part of the stream. If they fly upstream of the chalk bags, they might be laying their eggs in a bed of acid.

Apparently it came as a surprise to many people that this would happen, but my guess is, that's politics. If you want to build a road, you have to downplay the negative environmental impact and then just be ready to deal with it when it comes. They deal with this by forcing the streams to run through bags of limestone, which will help to raise the pH again, but it's an imperfect solution. Whatever is upstream of the bags will be unaffected; and it's difficult to place the bags in the right locations, or in the right quantities to account for seasonal changes of water levels. Still, at least they're trying. Eventually, Spring Creek's waters will lick its own wounds and heal the harm we have done, just as Bald Eagle Mountain will one day let its wounds scab over with oxidized stones, grasses and trees, and topsoil. But probably not in my lifetime.

TRANSPLANTS AND STOCKED FISH

A few years ago I took a job in South Dakota. My kids and I, having lived in places with many streams, now joke that the Big Sioux River that flows through the city we now live in has at least two falsehoods in its name: "big" and "river." One local quipped to me that the slow-moving, brown waters of the Big Sioux are "too muddy to drink and too wet to plow." I often miss the clear freestone streams of home, where my ancestors turned over rocks a thousand years ago and where Boey and I chased crayfish and trout as boys. I sometimes tell friends, wistfully, that "Dakota" means "land without trout streams." Of course, that isn't what the word means. It's also not true that there aren't any trout. Like me, trout are not native to the Dakotas, but they've been transplanted here and have found homes in streams in the Black Hills and a few other places, including one city pond in Sioux Falls.

Even though I miss the trout streams of my youth, I have a good job, with excellent people, and that's a lot to be thankful for. The Norwegian Lutherans who settled this part of the country know about gratitude, and they give thanks for all sorts of good things. My students often thank me at the end of the semester for the things I've taught them. That means more to me than words can easily say, and I, too, am learning gratitude.

My wife and I have moved a lot, though: from Vermont, where our first two children were born, to New Mexico, where our third was born, and from there to Pennsylvania and now here. I spent all my childhood in one home, the land of my foremothers and forefathers, but my kids have grown up all over the continent. What waters will they call home? Maybe they will be like the brown trout and rainbow trout of the Northeast: nonnative, but wild, flourishing, and free. I hope so.

The lines on the map are helpful fictions; they do not really exist in the world. Yes, they correspond to rivers and roads, but rivers and roads and mountains are not as firmly bounded as we might wish. Look closely at the edge of a road sometime, or the bank of a river. The plants beside the road are always slowly ripping apart the asphalt. As Heraclitus pointed out so long ago, the river itself changes from moment to moment, so that you really can't step in the same river twice. Most of the lines we think of as solid and firm become more vague the closer we look at them. Where does the mountain end and the valley begin? Where does one stream end as it pours into another? Where does one generation end, and the next begin? And when exactly does recess end?

I don't have answers to most of these questions, but I keep looking for them. My father once said that if I followed the streams I'd find my way. So I keep following them. In looking back over what I have written in this chapter I see that a number of times I've said "I hand the rod to my son." Just as rods were handed to me by my father, just as concern for these waters has been handed to me by my ancestors, who knew the pulse of the river, the life cycles of the invertebrates living under its stones. This is the rhythm I want my children to learn.

Second Dam

On Dams

David O'Hara

"Gwnewch y pethau bychain" (Do the little things)
—a saying attributed to Saint David of Wales

A FEW MILES UPSTREAM from the town of Wisla on the Vistula River in southern Poland there is a dam. The dam was built when communism flourished in Poland, and its aesthetics reflect the taste of the day, with form following far behind function. It is not majestic or pretty, but it is fairly large for a small river like the southern Vistula, and it does its work of holding drinking water and generating electricity well.

Below the dam, the Vistula is a charming stream that runs the length of Wisla. Low concrete barriers stretch across the river every few hundred meters. The water drops over them a foot or two, making plunge pools deep enough for tourists from Poland's cities to escape the heat, and there anglers can cast flies for the abundant *pstrag*, or brown trout, that live in those waters.

To say that the summer of 1997 was a wet summer is to understate the facts. It rained constantly in the Beskidy Mountains that straddle the border between Poland and the Czech Republic. Each day brought heavy soaking rains, and when it was not pouring it was drizzling or spitting rain, the abundant overflow of heaven drenching the ground. All over central Europe rivers were high. Crops were underwater in Germany.

The rains were welcome at first. The water filled the reservoir and soaked the thirsty fields, foretelling abundance and ease in the months ahead and offering deep pools for swimmers and fishermen. But as the rain continued to fall, the town engineers began letting more and more water through the dam. Even more rain fell, and they opened the floodgates completely—and still the water behind the dam rose. Throughout the town, anxiety grew, and one imagines that guilty consciences began to gnaw in many homes. Here's why:

My friend Ewa, who lives in Poland, stood beside the swollen river with me as we watched the boiling brown current shoot under the bridge. She told me that when the dam was built, there was not much money to pay the workers. The workers' paradise that had been promised had not yet been realized, and so many of the workers began to take their promised wages in the form of building materials from the worksite, in order to build homes for their families in Wisla. I'm told that in communist Europe people used to say, "We pretend to work, and the government pretends to pay us." If they could not earn wages, they would take what the wages were intended to buy, and the concrete appeared to be abundant enough that if a worker took a few bags home it wouldn't make a great difference for the dam but it would make all the difference for the worker who could now build a proper home. The engineers compensated for the losses by redesigning the dam to be a little thinner than planned, and a little weaker at the edges. Since dams are usually overengineered, there is some flexibility in the design, and as long as the dam isn't completely full, a thinner dam will hold just as well as the dam that was originally intended.

Only now the dam was full, and the whole town was contemplating the karmic irony that the homes built below the dam might soon be washed away. Had the materials gone into making the dam and not the homes, the dam would certainly hold, but the people would have no homes. As things stood, they had homes but now their hopes of keeping the homes diminished.

As people everywhere do when all their other hopes have fled, the people of Wisla began to pack up their photographs and heirlooms, and they began to pray. What else can be done in such situations?

Perhaps the weather simply responded to natural forces already in motion; perhaps heaven heard their cries. We cannot say why, but the rains slowed. The water behind the dam began to go down, and the town breathed a collective sigh of relief.

And so it is with dams. Dams hold tremendous promise, and equally tremendous peril. Below dams on the Winooski River in Vermont kayakers can experience daily whitewater conditions that would otherwise be only seasonally available to them. Because the water that goes through hydroelectric generators usually comes from the bottom of dams, the water downstream from dams tends to be cold and well-oxygenated, creating micro-ecosystems that would not otherwise exist on those rivers and contributing to the biodiversity of the watersheds. Turbines churn the biomass that flows into them, making a rich slurry of food for fish just downstream. The San Juan River in New Mexico flows through blistering desert, but for three miles below the Navajo Dam the water is a constant 39 degrees Fahrenheit and so rich with insect life and algae that the river supports something like twenty thousand brown and rainbow trout per mile, making it a world-class fishery that boosts the local fishing economy and provides clean water and great outdoor recreation for tens of thousands of people both above and below the dam. Dams on the Columbia River have allowed eastern Oregon and Washington to develop agriculture where none was possible before, and the Columbia has become a playground with some of the best windsurfing and parasailing in the world. Huge sturgeon drift along the bottom; trees stand at attention in neat rows in artificial forests in eastern Oregon, growing fast on irrigated land and awaiting their imminent harvest, a bumper crop where once there was only desert. Residents of cities like Portland and Vancouver have all the water they could ever want, and the same dams that hold the water harvest the tug of gravity and turn its oceanward slide into clean, abundant, and renewable electricity.

But the people of Wisla know, as everyone who lives downstream of a dam knows, that the benefits of dams come at a price. Damming a river can be like putting a leash and collar on a sleeping bear. Sooner or later it will raise its head, and it will go where it wants to go, quite possibly taking its "master" with it. Rivers are not mastered; they tolerate our attempts to sequester them, but their patience with our folly has its limits.

And we have sequestered more than a few of them. In Vermont alone, there are more than twelve hundred dams, ranging from large hydroelectric installations to small concrete barriers installed by farmers a century ago to provide power for their farms or water for their animals. In North Carolina, there are over four thousand dams, most of which are privately owned. The other Appalachian states host comparable numbers of dams. All told, the United States has tens of thousands of dams, and over half a million miles of rivers and streams are impounded by them. And no dam is ever completely innocuous. Dams change ecosystems, both above and below the dams. They make some things possible that were not possible before, but they also bring other things to an end. Small dams built for irrigation in eastern Colorado are responsible for the disappearance of more than one unique species of fish that live nowhere else. As of just a few years ago, the Rio Grande no longer reaches the Gulf of Mexico, but dries up just a few yards short of the sea, its waters having been depleted by irrigation and urban uses upstream. It's the same story with the Colorado River. The mighty flood that carved the Grand Canyon is siphoned dry before it reaches the Gulf of California. The ecology of the Missouri River as it flows through the Dakotas is dependent upon annual flooding from Montana snowmelt. The dams that control that flooding do so by releasing less water in flood stage and more water in the dry season, keeping even water levels year-round. As a result, the gravel bars in the river don't experience the churning renewal that floodwaters once brought, and species like the sturgeon and paddlefish, whose reproductive fires are stoked by floodwaters and who need those long, fresh gravel bars for their love nests, cannot hear the voice of nature calling them to swim together in piscine caress and so to renew themselves. Sometimes we can reverse or mitigate the damage. The Army Corps of Engineers tries to release a big surge of water each year now from those dams on the Missouri to help the paddlefish get their mojo back. Where a few fish have survived, they can sometimes be enticed to spring back. But in perhaps half of their former range, like the lakes of western Iowa and some waterways that flowed from the Appalachians, they are now completely gone.

Thoreau knew already in the middle of the nineteenth century how important it was to spend time in the wilderness in order to be able to see more clearly what was lost as forests were felled and rivers polluted. During one river trip in southern New Hampshire, he wrote,

> Salmon, shad, and alewives were formerly abundant here, and taken in weirs by the Indians, who taught this method to the whites, by whom they were used as food and as manure, until the dam and afterward the canal at Billerica, and the factories at Lowell,

put an end to their migrations hitherward. . . . Perchance, after a few thousands of years, if the fishes will be patient, and pass their summers elsewhere meanwhile, nature will have leveled the Billerica dam, and the Lowell factories, and the Grass-ground River run clear again, to be explored by new migratory shoals, even as far as the Hopkinton pond and Westborough swamp.[7]

If only it were so. Salmon and trout are *anadromous* (from Greek words meaning "upwards running"). Each year they, too, follow the summons of nature and race upstream to the waters they originated from, following some deep osmic memory to find their source and to repeat the process of making their species new again. Salmonids are known for their tenacity and their ability to leap high barriers to find those places. Some trout and salmon have been known to leap into and swim through narrow drainpipes in search of home when the original stream has been diverted through culverts. But dams are often insuperable barriers, and when salmonids are unable to reach their spawning grounds in their home river, they will vanish from that river entirely, taking with them the unique genetic strains that have evolved to match that home. Great runs of Atlantic salmon used to spawn in the upper reaches of the Connecticut River that separates Vermont from New Hampshire. The nineteenth and twentieth centuries brought dams to the river, to harness the free power that courses in its veins. But those dams cut off the salmon from their natal redds, and despite the introduction of fish ladders and other attempts to restore them, the salmon have never returned in significant numbers. Perchance, after a few thousands of years . . .

Chapter 3

The South Holston and Wild Southern Brook Trout

Matthew Dickerson

Watching was my Harvard and my Yale. It took a long time to discover just what was happening in the water, and I am not sure I really have it yet. Surely, I have learned a trick or two and know the names of a few insects, and I have learned something about the length of leaders and the thickness, too, but all of this, which I learned so slowly and with such effort, came from watching.

—CRAIG NOVA, *BROOK TROUT AND THE WRITING LIFE*[8]

I STAND IN THE South Fork of the Holston River. I have finished putting together all the sections of my eight-piece L. L. Bean travel fly rod, making a nine-foot long instrument out of a tube full of individual pieces short enough to fit in my briefcase or carry-on bag. I love the rod not only because its convenient size makes it possible to turn any of my otherwise less exciting business trips into an opportunity for a fishing outing, but because it casts as smoothly and powerfully as any two-piece or four-piece rod I have used. But there is always that two-minute period at the start of a day when, eager to be on the river, I wish for fewer sections. Two minutes that seem like an eternity.

The rod is designed to cast 5-wt fly line, which is a standard line for general purpose trout fishing. It would not suffice for a day of salmon or steelhead fishing. For that I want something heavier that can cast larger flies and has the power to turn a big fish. And on the other end, on my many excursions up some tiny Appalachian stream I want a shorter and lighter rod. For this river, though, it should be just right. It will not take much effort to get a fly across the river or far enough upstream to fish a pool without spooking it. I don't expect to hook any fish capable of breaking it. Though I can always hope for a fish that big.

It was no trivial engineering feat to design and build a rod with so many junctions that casts as smoothly and with the same sensitivity as a one- or two-piece rod, and with only imperceptibly more weight. And indeed, it may well be an indictment of our society that enough people travel on airplanes with enough regularity that a company would devote considerable effort to making an eight-piece rod so smooth and strong that I use it even when not traveling. But the fact is I do enough travel for my job and my writing, and I like to have a fly rod with me most places I go, that I am appreciative of the effort. I have another multipiece L. L. Bean travel rod in an 8-wt size for when I travel to salmon and steelhead waters.

Today I am casting what I consider small flies. With fly lines, a larger number means heavier line. A 7-wt line has more mass foot-for-foot than a 5-wt line, which has more mass than a 3-wt line. Same goes for fly rods, which are numbered for the weight line they are designed for. When it comes to leaders, tippet, and flies, however, the system is reversed—a scheme that is rather counter-intuitive and even confusing at first! A #8 hook is smaller than a #4 hook. A #20 hook is much smaller still. A #20 fly could easily rest on the nail of a pinky finger, and if it falls off into the carpet there is a good chance you will lose it until somebody walks around barefoot. Similarly with tippet, a larger number means a small diameter. Tippets for fly fishing generally range from 0x, the largest, down to a very fine 7x, though some companies make tippet even smaller than that, in an 8x or 9x. The smaller numbered and larger sized tippets have the advantage of being stronger, but the disadvantages of being both more visible to a fish and also too large to fit through the eye of a small fly. It is generally the case that smaller flies, clearer water, and warier trout all require smaller tippets of size 5x, 6x, or even 7x. It is easy enough to break 7x tippet that I sometimes do it accidentally when tying on a fly. Bigger trout require heavier tippet. When fishing for salmon or steelhead I use something in the range from

0x for king salmon down to 2x for smaller salmon or steelhead. Of course sometimes one ends up fishing for large fish that are also wary, are living in clear water, and eating small flies; that's when the real challenge begins.

I am fishing with nymphs of size #16 down to #20. A size #16 fly is like the size of a mosquito. A size #20 fly is like a black fly or midge. These are small enough that I need my magnifying glasses to tie them on. By necessity, my leader and tippet is fine and light. My main section of leader ends with 6x tippet, and I have a section of 7x connecting my first fly to the dropper. It takes no more than a little tug with my hands—or a good head shake from a strong fish—to break this.

The day is gray and overcast. The trees along the shoreline are barren of leaves, and it is their gray bark that now stands out. It is January and there was frost on the ground when the day started. Now, in the late morning, it might be as warm as 45 degrees, though I have not bothered to check. I am keeping warm enough. Along with my jacket I have on a fleece headband, fleece fishing gloves, and wool-blend long underwear beneath my waders. I wade in water only to the tops of my calves. A few small yellow mayflies have begun to emerge. When I see them, I switch my dropper fly from a midge to a yellowish bead-head hare's ear nymph. The result of the switch is a hungry rainbow trout. This is the Holston at its finest.

Tennessee fisheries biologist Jim Habrera speaks of the South Fork of the Holston River as the "best managed wild trout stream" in the state. Two different fishing guides I spoke with confirmed that assessment. It is a few days after my trip to the South Holston that I interview Habrera, and he tells me of a recent population survey done with electroshocking in which a brown trout measuring forty-one inches and probably weighing around thirty-six pounds turned up, was measured and catalogued, and then released. This gets my attention. If I had known in advance about that fish, I might have brought a heavier rod and spent the morning fishing with considerably stronger tippet. But my conversation with Habrera does not take place until after my first morning on the South Holston. And so, as with so many of the Appalachian streams and rivers Dave and I have explored—especially those outside the Northeast—I had little idea what to expect on that January day in 2009 when I visited the river for the first time.

I had fished the main stem of the Holston once before, in late May of the previous year, when Dave and I were on our way from the Tellico River in Tennessee to the Cumberland in Kentucky. We chose a route that took us in the general vicinity of the Cherokee Dam, near Jefferson City, east-northeast of Knoxville. We made the detour off the main highway and stopped for a few casts in the tailwater stretch of the Holston directly below the dam. We arrived in the early afternoon, plied our waders over our bodies, fished for two hours in waist-deep slow current, and caught a handful of trout on dry flies. We scurried out of the river when there was a release from the dam and the water began to rise.

That excursion was about a hundred miles downriver of Bristol, well below the confluence of the South Fork with the main stem of the Holston. Below the Cherokee Dam the Holston River may contain some proportion of water that once flowed down a forested mountain somewhere, but it has none of the character of an Appalachian river. No peaks are visible from its shoreline. Only the dam itself towered over us like a small mountain. We were casting amidst the shadows, not of pine or spruce or oak, but of the concrete pylons from the overpass that spanned the river just upstream of where we stood in the water. It was a nice break from the driving, a chance to be in the water casting a fly line and perhaps to land a few trout, probably freshly stocked. It was pleasant enough if I focused my attention on the water and the insects, and on my casting, and not on the concrete pylon forest or the concrete mountain. Even in a place like that, there is a soothing rhythm to the casting of a fly rod. After several days fishing mostly small Appalachian streams in North Carolina and Tennessee, in the Nantahala and the Cherokee national forests, it was nice to be in open water with no branches overhead, and to be able to feel the rod load and unload as I laid out the full fifty or sixty feet of line the rod is designed to cast. It was pleasant to watch the loop unfold in front of me, to see a Wulff or elk hair caddis land on a flat surface, and to see the roll of a head as a rainbow came up to sip in the meal. Or, as often as not, to see the fish turn away at the last moment. It was decent fishing, and we had the place to ourselves. It was almost possible to ignore the traffic overhead and the concrete mountain devoid of trees.

But what memory could I draw on to prepare for my trip to the South Holston? Prior to the January morning on the South Fork of the Holston, I'd done little winter fishing in the southern Appalachians. The closest I had come were two days in late February with my brother Ted on the Little Tennessee and the Cheoah rivers in North Carolina, at their confluence near the Tennessee border. But both the Little Tennessee and the Cheoah, as anybody who knows them will attest, are very different rivers from the

South Fork of the Holston in Bristol. They differ in size and in character and in the surrounding landscape. Neither my numerous prior visits to those rivers nor my one visit to Cherokee Dam told me anything about what the South Holston might be like where it flows through an Appalachian valley on a winter day. To guide my expectations that January morning as I drove toward Bristol, I had only sketchy notes from interviews and phone conversations with fishing guides and biologists, plus a few brief descriptions and photos from printed guidebooks and websites. The photos didn't show much of the river or the backdrop. They showed anglers kneeling in the water holding fish and smiling. Like many fly-fishing photos, they could have been taken anywhere. So I could conjure up no mental picture of the river as I pulled a rental minivan out of the Super 8 motel in Morristown at 7:30 a.m. and started east in on I-81 in the wake of the SUV of our soon-to-be fishing guide, Rocky—whom I'd also never met until we shook hands in the motel lobby.

With me that morning were two Middlebury College students, Kelly March and Connor Wood. Both were sophomore environmental studies majors whose primary interest was in the creative writing aspect of the major. They had taken a course with me the previous spring titled "Essay Writing on Nature and Ecology." This trip was, for them, part of a follow-up independent study course: "Trout and the Ecology of the Appalachians." It was mostly a chance for them to write about ecological issues. Neither of them had any experience fly fishing. And if either managed to catch a trout, that would also be a first. Both had more or less urban backgrounds. Connor was from north of Chicago. Kelly—though she had roots and family in West Virginia—was currently living in Boston. So their mental picture of the river was probably even dimmer than mine.

What we did have were maps. And we had looked at them closely. Both the North Fork and South Fork of the Holston have headwaters in the western corner of Virginia where five Appalachian states come almost, but not quite, together. The stretch of the Virginia Appalachians is nestled between Kentucky on the west, West Virginia to the north, Tennessee to the southwest, and North Carolina to the southeast. Here the spur of the Appalachians runs almost forty-five degrees northeast, really more east than north. Its path is followed by several parallel river valleys separated by ridgelines, with all the rivers flowing southwest from Virginia into Tennessee. The South Fork is the easternmost of these as it crosses into Tennessee near the large border town of Bristol, where each year hundreds of thousands of people converge to watch auto racing. Then comes the North Fork, followed by the Clinch and the Powell rivers.

As noted, the area that is home to this handful of rivers is not large. From the corner where Tennessee, North Carolina, and Virginia come together it is only about forty miles due north to the border of West Virginia. A crow would have to fly only about thirty miles to get from the North Fork to the Kentucky state line. The beautiful Cumberland Gap bounds the west side of this portion of Virginia. It is there that the mighty Cumberland River has its headwaters in a little stream called Martin's Fork, which flows out of the gap eastward, then north, and finally back again to the west.

All told, east to west, it is only about sixty miles from where the South Fork of the Holston crosses into Tennessee to the Cumberland Gap and Martin's Fork. These two bounding waters—the South Fork of the Holston and the Cumberland—are Appalachian-born waters with interesting stories about trout, and about brook trout, and about the lack of brook trout. Though, like the waters themselves, which start close together but flow in opposite directions, the stories are widely divergent.

But my stories of those rivers, like the story of the restoration of native brook trout in the South, will be slow in unfolding. It took me many days of fishing in the South, spread over many years, before I finally reached the famed South Fork of the Holston. Which is to say, the story has its diversions just like many of the rivers inhabiting it, but also like those rivers it is fishable water.

Though I am a New Englander and have done most of my fishing in the Northeast, I also have chased trout, and especially wild trout, and most especially wild brook trout, across the Southeast. My introduction to fly fishing in the Southeast came through my brother Ted and his sons Michael and Brad, during the decade or so they lived in western North Carolina. Much of it was in tributaries of the Little Tennessee River that Dave and I would later fish together.

That whole region of western North Carolina is an area of strange contrasts. Even in February, the Little Tennessee below the towering Cheoah Dam that impounds the Cheoah Reservoir looks and feels more like bass water. Though it is narrow with a visible current where it comes out of the bottom of Cheoah Dam, it soon becomes sluggish and enters another impoundment: a reservoir that straddles the North Carolina and Tennessee border at the end of that steep, narrowing valley passable only by boat. Yet the water had some aggressive and well-fed brook trout. After the warming morning air thawed out the frost on the sleeping bags where my brother and I had spent the night under the open sky, we cast streamer flies from a canoe and found the mouths of fish. They were the only brook trout I have caught in the Southeast greater than a foot in length. Though they were probably hatchery fish and of northern strain, they were still enjoyable to catch.

Just a long cast or three away from where I caught those brook trout is another fishable water. The Cheoah River flows into the Little Tennessee just below the Cheoah Dam. The Cheoah is a short river, but it is scenic and feels wild as it tumbles beside a road, falling quickly down a heavily wooded pass over the course of its fifteen-odd miles. It also bears the mark of human engineering. In some sense the Cheoah River "starts" at Lake Santeetlah. But to say that it starts at the lake is misleading. The water from Lake Santeetlah and its tributaries, which at one time flowed into the Cheoah River, is now diverted through pipelines down to generating turbines at the powerhouse below the dam. The Cheoah River directly below Lake Santeetlah is thus a dry riverbed. It must re-create its flow from a series of small tributaries that come off the steep hillsides and feed it along its short length. Amazingly, by the time it approaches the Little Tennessee, it has turned from a dry river once more into a passable trout stream tumbling over gravel, and often through a series of pools below many-ton boulders.

The nearby Nantahala River has a similar story. It flows north into and then out of Nantahala Lake and eventually joins the waters of the Little Tennessee upstream from the Cheoah at the head of Fontana Lake. In terms of the quality of fish and the habitat that supports them, the Nantahala is a justifiably famous trout stream. Fishing with Ted, I caught my first North Carolina trout in the Nantahala some years earlier. There are places even below the lake where the Nantahala River gives the impression of being a wild stream as it winds through steep terrain and a forested landscape. But most of the water that ought to come to it from its headwaters above Nantahala Lake also is diverted from the lake to the turbines in a power station many miles downriver. Thus the Nantahala River below the lake must also start again from scratch. It holds brook trout there, but they are stocked. It is better known for its brown and rainbow trout, which are also stocked to account for the heavy fishing pressure of a put-and-take fishery. Through the gorge and in the lowest stretch where kayakers come to run a permanent course laid out in the river at a famous outdoor center, it feels more like a playground than a wild trout stream. It was there I caught my first North Carolina trout. It was also there I had my first experience with a belligerent kayaker apparently opposed to fishing. She went several yards out of the course, and out of her way, just to harass me and drive me off the river, or at least drive away any fish that might be feeding around me.

Above its namesake lake, the Nantahala is a wild stream, and it is managed as one. Its smaller tributaries contain wild brook trout. Though too small to sustain any real fishing pressure involving the harvest of fish, the tributaries are important for these wild brookies, and hence for all of southern Appalachia.

It is upstream of Lake Santeetlah that the stories get even more interesting—both more frustrating and sad, and also more promising. My first day here years earlier began on Tulula Creek, a tributary of Lake Santeetlah that flows through the only major town in the area: Robbinsville. We fished the morning here with Ted's friend Scott, who is half Cherokee and whose ancestors have lived in the area for generations. Scott told stories of having snagged himself in the chest with big treble hooks and having to rip the hooks free. While Ted and I fished flies, working our way upstream from the lake all the way into the town, the more practical Scott fished worms. In a stream laden with discarded cars and appliances, Scott caught and kept the only fish: a small rainbow whose gullet was completely empty except for a discarded cigarette butt. Scott, Ted, and I then spent that afternoon just a few miles away on another tributary of the same lake, Big Snowbird Creek, which runs through the public land of the national forest. It was one of the prettiest and most pristine streams I have fished in the South, devoid of trash and rusting appliances. It was also the home of wild brook trout. The contrast between Snowbird and the nearby Tulula could not have been greater.

And this brings my tale almost back to the South Fork of the Holston, half a year after my trip with Dave to the Little Tennessee, and a few years after my trip with my brother Ted and his friend Scott to Tulula Creek. My lack of real personal, intimate knowledge of the South Fork did not in the slightest quell the enthusiasm I have when heading out to a trout stream with a fly rod. The famous stretch of the South Fork where we headed that morning is a tailwater fishery below the South Holston Dam. It boasts rainbows as well as browns, but the browns are its hallmark. More than a decade ago, surveys indicated that the brown trout were naturally reproducing. The state stopped stocking browns in the river, and the population has been self-sustaining since before the start of the new millennium. Rainbows also thrive in the river, with its abundance of food and well-oxygenated water. However, as one biologist told us, the river doesn't have spawning grounds well suited for rainbows, so they have to be replenished with stocking.

The abundant wild browns and the chance for trophy fish excited me as a fly fisherman. But there was even more to draw me not only as an angler but as someone interested in brook trout and in ecology. Like the Little Tennessee, the Cheoah, and the Nantahala rivers, the South Holston also has feeder tributaries coming out of higher ranges of the Appalachians containing wild brook trout. Habrera said that in Tennessee alone the South Holston had twenty-three tributaries up in the Smoky Mountain National Forest with populations of wild brook trout. Some of these now have the highest concentrations of wild brook trout anywhere in the South. And that is just in Tennessee. There are more tributaries and headwaters up in Virginia also holding brook trout. What was particularly interesting about the wild brook trout in South Fork tributaries was that these southern strain wild fish had not somehow miraculously persisted through the deforestation and introduction of nonnative fish, but rather were there because of a difficult and extensive effort to reintroduce them.

There are several obstacles to the restoration of native brook trout. One is the removal of invasive species, in this case rainbow trout. Electroshocking is one possible solution to this problem; applying a shocking current to the water stuns fish, which then float downstream. If the goal of the electroshocking is a survey, then the fish can be counted and released—after gaping in awe at any lunkers that turn up. But if the goal is the restoration of another fish, then the shocked fish can instead be removed from the water and killed, or transplanted elsewhere. Unfortunately, electroshocking devices have limited stunning range in the water. They are also heavy and nontrivial to haul up and down streams. Thus this approach, while successful in some places when done repeatedly, has been less effective in streams where the habitat is complex or the pools are large and deep.

A second approach is the use of fish toxicant to kill the rainbow trout. Studies on southern Appalachian streams have shown that this latter method is both less expensive and in general more effective at removing unwanted fish. Unfortunately, it involves dumping poison into the very water one is trying to restore to its natural state. There is something unnerving about this. Studies suggest that the impact of fish toxicants on aquatic life other than the targeted fish is minimal. That is, the mortality rate of aquatic invertebrates, crayfish, and amphibians is small enough to justify the approach given that the end result is the removal of a nonnative species and the restoration of a native one. These toxins quickly break down rather than remaining in the ecosystem. Nonetheless, the toxicant does unavoidably travel downstream, and it is hard to know whether we can predict all the effects of adding more toxins to the water. We can predict what we know to look for; but the history of ecology is so often the history of unanticipated effects.

One fishing guide we spoke with mentioned another approach that had supposedly been used on a few streams to remove the imported and unwanted rainbows: simply gather a group of willing anglers and sponsor a short but sustained period of intense fishing pressure designed to remove all the rainbows. He claimed the approach had been done with some success and at very little cost. I wanted to believe this; it is certainly the sort of fish restoration effort I would enjoy. It is also one that does not involve poisoning a river. How often have I been to an overfished put-and-take trout stream—the sort of place where other anglers come to fill their creels and freezers, and keep everything they catch—and spent a morning or evening fishing there, and gotten skunked? The answer is, more times than I would like to admit. We say the stream has been "fished out." Of course, it might not really have been completely fished out. Depending on the river, some few wary and leader-shy fish may have survived in a deep log-filled hole somewhere. Perhaps with enough fishing pressure over a long enough time it might eventually be freed of its inhabitants. But who wants to be the person who stays on fishing for three more nearly-but-not-quite-futile days to catch that very last fish that needs to be removed? And who knows which fish really is the very last fish? Still, though perhaps insufficient to remove all fish, intensive fishing may remove a breeding population of rainbows long enough to reestablish a breeding population of brook trout. So our guide told us. I'd like to believe him.

Of course, once the imported rainbows are gone from an area, barriers then need to be built to prevent them from returning. This is costly and usually requires a helpful geographic feature: a natural waterfall or even an artificial waterfall created by a culvert. Another complex problem is getting the wild southern strain brook trout into the stream once the rainbows are gone. Northern brook trout have been bred in hatcheries for decades. Attempts at breeding southern strain brookies, however, have been largely ineffective. The raceways of hatcheries where the fish are kept and fed their protein pellets are uniform concrete structures. They are streams only in the sense that water flows through them. I guess gravel bottoms, boulders, trees, and other debris that might make for a nice stream would also make a hatchery raceway more difficult to clean and maintain. It is not surprising that little wild southern brook trout kept in a raceway do not breed properly. It is more surprising that northern brook trout do.

Fortunately, one biologist working in the Tellico Hatchery near the Tellico River, using wild brook trout of the aboriginal strain taken from Bald River, was eventually successful in raising a brood of young fish to be stocked elsewhere. He simply added rocks and logs and other structure to the sterile concrete hatchery raceway to make it more like a stream. There is something very appealing about this approach. And it did work. It was also quite labor intensive. The Tellico Hatchery was the first and only hatchery ever to succeed at captive reproduction of southern Appalachian brook trout.

The method that eventually proved most successful and economic was to bypass the captive reproduction stage altogether and simply capture— again through electroshocking—a small number of fish from one wild and healthy population and transplant them to another. The fish lost from the donor river quickly repopulate their new home by natural breeding, generally within a year or two. The fish introduced (or restored) to the new water take more time to establish, but often as few as fifty fish are sufficient to re- claim the water for the native species. Thanks to several efforts of this type, and to the discovery of several waters still shown through genetic testing to contain some pure southern strain fish, wild brook trout have been restored and now thrive in many small tributaries of the South Fork and other rivers in the national forests and national parks of the South.

I've caught some of these surviving wild southern strain brookies, though not in the headwaters of the Holston where they were successfully restored. The places they survived are beautiful, and so are the fish. But we'll tell that story in a later chapter. Sometime I hope also to visit the tribu- taries of the Holston in the Smoky Mountains, where the restoration efforts have been successful. But whether I ever get there or not, I still delight to know that the trout exist in those places once more. I delight to know that mountains once stripped of their trees are again able to support such wild and beautiful fish—populations that are both surprisingly fragile and surprisingly resilient.

WHAT WE BREAK AND WHAT WE FIX

Those were places and memories my mind wandered to on the hour-plus drive up to Bristol as I followed Rocky's truck in my rental car. They were the bits of information about the area I would be fishing that had been filtered first by others, and then by me, consciously and unconsciously. It is also the end of the diversion: the place where the water flows back into the river bed and continues the journey down its original course. For all of this, like information about what insects can be found on the stretch of the South Fork where we would be fishing, is just book knowledge: facts one can get off a piece of paper. I didn't know what the stream was like: how wide or shallow it was, or what the surrounding landscape was like, or what the bottom was like. Was it slick? Gravelly? Silty? What were the banks like? Grassy? Wooded? Lots of trees? It was supposed to be an easily waded stream, and not readily floatable. But that could mean a lot of things. Recommendations from biologists and guides, the presence of the native brookies in various headwaters, and the promise of healthy browns and 'bows in the lower stretches made the Holston interesting for our project— interesting enough to justify an exploratory trip.

Some time when it was warmer, maybe I would get out my hiking shoes and short lightweight fly rod and try to find some of the tributaries with wild brookies up in the heart of the Appalachians. On this short January day, with morning temperatures below freezing, we would focus just on a small stretch of tailwater lower down in the valley, chasing browns and rainbows. The stretch we would fish had no lure restrictions, nor was it catch-and-release. And people fished it year-round. That left me a bit nervous that the river would be "fished out." What we had in our favor was a regulation protecting breeding-size fish. Fish between sixteen and twenty-two inches in length had to be released. This is known as a "slot limit," and it protects the fish during the period when they are at a peak of reproductive maturity. The state also closed some of the important spawning areas during spawning season to ensure that breeding fish would not be caught or even harassed. Furthermore, in January the fishing pressure would probably be lower thanks to the cold. With these protections in place, the chance of landing something even on a cold winter day was decent. At least I hoped so.

It was a misty drive. Not much was visible, but I was aware of a steady climb in elevation. That, at least, told me we were getting into the foothills of the Appalachians. We pulled off I-81 in the southwestern corner of the

Bristol area and stopped for gas. Then the mist lifted. Suddenly a snow-covered line of peaks opened up. Like many scenes of the Appalachians, it was stunningly beautiful—the type of view I do not tire of. It was also a strangely disconnected scene to witness while driving past Bristol Motor Speedway. The speedway is a place gouged out of the rolling hillsides with massive earthmoving machines. How does one make a mile or more of level ground in this terrain? Who envisioned putting a racetrack here? It is a place that is about loud noise, speed, and human engineering.

I am not a car racing fan. I admit that the appeal of the sport eludes me. I know next to nothing about NASCAR. *Cars* and its sequel are the only Pixar films I have not seen. I have heard that auto racing is the number one spectator sport in the United States. I do have enough friends who love racing that I must assume there is something exciting about it; I must assume that my own lack of appreciation arises from a shortcoming in myself. But my impression, right or wrong, is that this big racetrack in the middle of nowhere is a place where most of the fans are entirely unaware of wild brook trout, and are in most cases not there to enjoy the nearby snow-covered mountains or the beauty of a trout stream.

I am even tempted toward a sort of judgmental attitude toward racing when I consider the massive amount of petroleum and other resources that must be consumed at every major race—not just the fuel burned in the high-horsepower automobiles that zip around the track, but the resources consumed in the manufacture of the cars and stadium, and the fuel used to bring all the fans to the track. It is this last thought that brings me up short, and causes a quick and guilty end to my condemning thoughts. Our guide Rocky and I have just driven two cars sixty some miles so that I could spend a day fishing here. How many more miles will I put on the car fishing over the next week? How many on the plane to get here? I don't want to think about this. If the racing fans are guilty, so am I. It's easy to assign blame for environmental problems to others—unless one is honest and equitable. I quickly busy my mind thinking about the river again. What will the fishing be like?

We arrive at the river at 9:00 a.m. It is a winter day and fish will not be biting until the sun starts warming up the water, so there was and still is no rush to get to the river or to get onto the water. A morning like this is not the sort of morning on which the extra two minutes to put together an eight-piece rod should bother me—although it still does.

Downstream

When my rod is together and lined, I pause to look around. What I notice first is how strange the river is. How unnatural it looks. It is almost as engineered as the speedway. We are downstream of a hydroelectric dam—a seventy-some-year-old earthenwork dam operated by the Tennessee Valley Authority. Although the dam is just out of sight upstream around a bend, I am aware that we will be fishing a tailwater. I have always associated tailwater rivers with cold, well-oxygenated trout habitat. I thought that was a universal: an unavoidable but fortuitous by-product of large dams. Tailwaters are why one can find great trout fishing even in hot and arid areas of Texas, New Mexico, and Arizona as well as hot and humid Southeastern states. But the connection of tailwaters with good trout fisheries is not a given, and I learn something new from our guide.

Warm water in the reservoir above the South Holston Dam actually keeps oxygen from reaching the depths where the cold water could absorb it. And so, although the water comes through the turbines cold and capable of carrying a healthy amount of the dissolved oxygen necessary for cold-water species like trout, in this case it is actually oxygen-deficient. Despite the cold, trout could not live in the water below the dam. Furthermore, this dam has a regular release schedule of just a couple hours of generation per day. Then the release is shut off. This results in a short period of very high river flow, followed by almost no water at all. If the lack of oxygen were not fatal to trout, the lack of water would be.

And so a solution was engineered. Downstream of the hydro dam is a strange sluice or dam full of holes, called a labyrinth weir. It looked to be no more than twenty feet tall. But it is a long sluice with a significant storage capacity. And a few hundred yards below that is a long metal grate stretching across the river. During the brief generating period when water is released from the big hydro dam, it gets captured by the holding area above the weir. From there it pours down slowly through the small holes up on the sides of the weir making for a relatively steady flow throughout the day, even when the turbines are not running. I'd never seen a dam set up like this. Pouring through the holes in the weir also oxygenates the water like a waterfall would. The water is then further oxygenated downstream as it rushes over a grate that creates a sort of artificial riffle. All of this results in a relatively steady supply of cold, well-aerated water—nearly perfect trout habitat, at least for brown trout. There is also tremendous and varied insect life, even in January.

But my mind is spinning. Did the dam destroy fish habitat or create it? Is human engineering to blame or to credit? Are all these dams and weirs and grates creating problems or solving them? Or both?

When we arrive there are three or four other anglers already fishing at the grate. By lunchtime, there will be nine total. A few are fellow fly casters. Others are fishing with bait and spinners. But the grate is wide and the pool below it is large. There is plenty of space for all of us. And more importantly, there are also hundreds of small brown trout rising steadily all day after midges. Mixed in are a few big hogs that come up to the surface and roll, causing our hearts to thump before they disappear back into the depths. All the anglers—fly casters, bait fishermen, lure casters—are regularly catching fish. The fly fishermen are releasing them. Others are putting them on stringers or in coolers to bring home for supper. They are mostly browns from a wild, though not indigenous, self-sustaining population. Most are in the eight-to-twelve-inch range. A few anglers walk off with fourteen-to-sixteen-inch fish. I do not see any thirty-six pounders or even any three-pounders.

Our guide, Rocky, is a big man. He is at least 6 feet 4 inches tall. But he is intimidating in size only. He proves very genial, and eager to get Connor and Kelly their first trout and their first fish on a fly. He has us all tie on a size #18 pheasant tail nymph with a #20 zebra midge below it as a dropper. Then he sends me off downstream on my own so that he can concentrate his efforts on helping the rookies.

I am glad to be away from the crowd at the grate. Around the corner, away from the bridge and out of the trees, vistas of the mountains with snow-covered peaks once more open up before me to the east. It is a lovely landscape, and feels more Appalachian. I can ignore the jarring incongruity of the grate, the weir, the dam. There are no anglers downstream of me for a hundred yards or more. The fishing is not fast and furious, but for January it isn't bad. I land a half dozen fish, mostly on nymphs. All but one are browns. I return to the bridge for lunch. I learn that Connor has landed one rainbow and three browns. Kelly has landed three rainbows and one brown. I congratulate them. Their faces and words register their delight. They also communicate the frustrations of somebody learning to wield a fly rod. Fortunately, working from the grate does not require much in the way of real fly casting. For lunch Rocky serves us hot soup and tuna salad. The soup goes down nicely on a January day. Since we release all the trout we catch, the tuna is the only fish we eat.

In the afternoon some bigger insects hit the water. There is lots of grassy land around the river. Though it is winter, I have seen some terrestrial insects near the river. In colder climates, where I have done much more of my fly fishing, I usually use grasshoppers only in the late summer and early fall when they are abundant. But this is the South. I decide to try on a small grasshopper imitation anyway. I land a fourteen-inch brown. It is my largest fish of the day. Though I see a few tails, lips, and backs of larger fish, I do not land any. But I become more aware of one other aspect of the river. It is a by-product of the dam and weir-controlled flow and the resulting lack of any of the river-bottom scouring action that would come from ice or simply high spring runoff. It is a by-product also of the fact that anglers come from all over the world to fish here, and bring with them bits and pieces of whatever river they last fished stuck to the bottom of their waders and felt soles. It is a by-product of the presence of people like me, and the fact that rod-makers have a market for travel fly rods that fit inside luggage.

The bottom of the South Fork of the Holston is covered with *Didymosphenia geminata*, the invasive algae known more commonly as didymo. This is the first place I have fished that is significantly overrun with the stuff. To the frustration of various state biologists I have spoken with, didymo is also commonly referred to as "rock snot." It is an inaccurate name; the algae, far from feeling slick and slimy, forms a sort of carpet that provides decent footing. It obviously has not destroyed the fishing. I have read that while didymo is detrimental to some sorts of aquatic insects, other insects are not bothered by it and some may even be helped. Whether it affects the quality of rainbow trout spawning habitat, I don't know. But it does not seem to inhibit brown trout reproduction, and whatever it has done to the insect population is not readily visible in the air.

In any case, most of the river bottom is covered with didymo. As I admitted above, it makes for decent footing. But it is ugly. I will need to be careful at the end of the day to sterilize my wading shoes so that I do not become guilty of spreading it. And maybe now the picture that at first felt incongruous is incongruous only with my romantic imagination. The dam. The weir. The grate. The browns, now acclimated and self-sustaining but still imported and nonindigenous. The stocked rainbows whose population could not even continue without human intervention. The didymo. This is an environment heavily engineered and impacted by humans. Is the Bristol Motor Speedway up the road all that different?

Up in the hills, wild brook trout streams had been destroyed by logging and stocking. Creative humans had found a way, in part through chemicals and sometimes through earth-moving machines, but also through intimate knowledge and hard work, to restore those streams. Now they once again have healthy populations of wild and even aboriginal trout in the midst of healthy forests. Down in the valley, the South Fork of the Holston, which had likely never historically been a good coldwater fishery, had become a trophy trout fishery. But it took more than a hydro dam alone to accidentally create good trout habitat. A great deal of additional engineering had to be done. And the creation of a top-notch trout stream brought its own problems in the form of didymo. I am still not sure what to think of all this, as an angler drawn as much to the wildness of rivers as to the trout that inhabit them, who does love to catch a big fish now and then but who also cares about ecology and nature independent of the presence of trout and the pleasure they bring.

Still I want to return and fish here again. I would enjoy catching that thirty-six pound brown. But I would also just enjoy fishing in a place where that brown can put just a little edge on every cast, and where I would actually be thrilled to catch a trout even one-tenth that weight. Even more, I want to head upstream into the mountains and fish Sam's Creek or another of the many tributaries where wild brook trout now roam again out of sight of dams and weirs and grates and didymo. But it is January. Today was a warm day by the standards of winter fishing. There are no guarantees for tomorrow.

Third Dam

The Dam We Call Home

Matthew Dickerson

He had wet his hand before he touched the trout, so he would not disturb the delicate mucus that covered him. If a trout was touched with a dry hand, a white fungus attacked the unprotected spot. Years before when he had fished crowded streams, with fly fishermen ahead of him and behind him, Nick had again and again come on dead trout, furry with white fungus, drifted against a rock, or floating belly up in some pool. Nick did not like to fish with other men on the river. Unless they were of your party, they spoiled it.

—ERNEST HEMINGWAY, "BIG TWO-HEARTED RIVER"

IT CAN TAKE A lifetime to get to know a river. For my first ten years in Vermont, I lived within a short walk of the New Haven River, and for the next thirteen years I lived only two miles away. In the flood of 1998, I could hear the New Haven rushing past with enough force to wash out an adjacent section of road. I spent the next year mourning the flood-caused loss of some favorite trout-friendly holes while also discovering several newly created ones. I think of the river in three distinct sections. There is an upper headwater portion in the town of Lincoln that is archetypal Vermont brook trout water. This is followed by a short steep section that plunges down a narrow defile from Lincoln to Bristol and eventually over Bartlett Falls into a popular swimming hole. And finally there is a lower and slower section about six miles long running to its confluence with Otter Creek.

My heart is most drawn to the smaller and more remote stretches inhabited by brook trout and sitting in the shadow of Vermont's fourth highest peak. However, the final section, dominated by stocked rainbow and brown trout, is the section I fish the most because it is closest to where I live. In the lower river there is also always a chance of hooking into a holdover trout that will bend my rod. I have caught a few fish there measured in pounds rather than inches. Occasionally a really big monster moves upstream into the New Haven from the much slower and larger Otter Creek. One of these, running at least two and half feet long, once spent about three seconds tail dancing at the end of my line. I think of it when I fish the lower river. But I fish all the sections from time to time, and I have favorite runs and pools in each.

Along a few stretches of the New Haven I have an intimate knowledge of the bends and patterns and character of the river. I could say the same about Otter Creek and the Middlebury River, the other two local rivers I most habitually fish. I belong to a fishing club named after the New Haven River. The club members consider the same group of rivers to be their home waters. The club gets together every month to talk about fishing. Granted that some of the other members know the New Haven far better than I, either because they have been fishing it for more years than the two decades I have put in, or because they have more time to fish, or perhaps just because they are better anglers. By and large, though, we all know most of the same holes and can refer to them with a word or two. Sometimes we fish together by choice. More often we just meet by chance on the local streams. When I landed a spawning thirty-one-inch landlocked salmon in another local river one October when the leaves were bright on the maples, I made no mention of the location in my biweekly fishing column. Nonetheless at least three members of the club knew exactly where I had caught the fish because we had met and exchanged pleasantries on the stream a few days earlier.

Oddly enough, many of the best and more famous rivers that Dave and I fished while writing this book do not seem to be the "home rivers" of many anglers. At least they were not home to the anglers we met on the stream. There are, of course, professional guides who know the famous rivers well, and we are grateful to several of them for the immensely helpful bits of knowledge they shared with us. But for many of them the river is a place of work, not a home. They rarely get a chance to fish the rivers where they work. Their knowledge is a professional or commercial one. And even the most knowledgeable of guides, out of necessity, usually work a number of rivers, often hours apart.

Mostly on our travels Dave and I met anglers who—like us—had come from afar. That is the nature of famous trout streams. Some of these anglers, decked out in their new Orvis attire, carrying rods by Sage and Winston and G. Loomis, seem to bounce from one famous hole to the next, from one river to another, even one state to another. It is difficult to imagine gaining a real, intimate knowledge of one local river from such an approach.

RUDE GUIDES AND A SENSE OF PLACE

One particular encounter stands out. Dave and I and my nephew Michael take a trip to a slightly more remote stretch of the Magalloway, above Aziscohos Lake but below Parmachenee Lake. We park just above the Aziscohos where the dirt road crosses the Magalloway. Michael fishes near the bridge. Dave and I walk upstream some distance, headed for the famous pool below the snowmobile bridge. At the tail of the pool I hook a good-sized fish on a black wooly bugger, but get broken off before I get a good look at it. I did feel the hit and the hard pulses of several head tosses before one big shake broke the line. I guess it was a lunker brookie. With 5x tippet, the fish should not have broken my line. Unless it was really big. Or unless the tippet had been nicked on the rock. In any event, I grow excited.

Over the next hour, though, we collectively land only about six big chubs, and Dave breaks off a fly on another large fish. We don't see any brook trout. Now, chubs are native fish. They belong in the water as much as brookies. We try not to hate them just because they are not trout. But it is frustrating to catch chubs when one is casting for trout. They are not a beautiful fish, and they don't put up much of a fight. It is not the six chubs, however, that make the experience a sour one. It isn't the lost flies either, though that is frustrating. It isn't even the steady cold rain that has begun to fall. (Our lunches and thermoses are back in the car.) It is certainly not the two big lost fish. Catching and losing fish is part of fishing. Knowing a hole contains a big fish adds to the excitement.

What makes the experience a sour one is the guide who suddenly appears, walking in on the snowmobile trail with three clients. The four of them strut out onto the bridge with a loud clomping of their booted feet.

We are in the pool fishing when they arrive. Admittedly, the pool is big enough maybe for three people to fish, if they are good friends and if they are polite. Though one person alone could actually easily fish the entire pool in five minutes. This is not the lower Magalloway where the stream is wide enough to offer room for many anglers to fish a single pool. The stream is small here. It is easily shallow enough to wade, and in most places narrow enough to cross in three or four steps. In fact, standing in the right place, one person could cast to the entire pool without moving. The current might make it hard to give your fly the right drift through the whole length of the pool, but it could be done.

In any case, there is a long-standing etiquette among fly casters. Standing in the backwoods of Maine we may be muddy and scruffy, smelling of a mix of sweat and bug repellent, and with the table manners of a sow bear in an ant nest, but we are still a politely respectful bunch when it comes to river manners. The etiquette and respect dictates that an angler does not enter an already occupied pool without asking permission. And a group of four people does not enter an occupied pool under any circumstances. Especially not with a good deal of open river downstream and literally miles of open river upstream, and not a single angler in sight in either direction.

This guide, however, does not ask permission, or even acknowledge our presence. He just crashes down into the water with three clients, and positions them around the upper end of the pool, close enough that we can smell the coffee on their breath. Suddenly, instead of two of us there are six, five of whom are fishing.

A moment earlier we had been ready go back to the car. The air is bitter. The rain is almost sleet. We are not warm. Instead of leaving, however, Dave and I look at each other and a common understanding passes between us without words. We hold our ground and continue to fish. Had the guide made even a small effort to be polite, we would have gladly yielded and made a beeline to our dry car and warm drinks. After all, any trout that might have been in the pool when we arrived were certainly driven into hiding by the commotion of five anglers. Instead, we stubbornly fish forty more minutes until the guide, frustrated by our persistence in holding our ground and probably even more frustrated by the lack of any fish being caught, finally calls his clients out of the stream and heads off down the trail.

Forty minutes of standing in the cold rain, catching nothing, aware of our own stubbornness as well as our discomfort, but unwilling to act on the knowledge. As soon as the guide and his clients are out of sight, we bolt downstream toward the car.

Now, we've been angling all our lives. We have put in many long hours on a variety of waters all over the country. We've both even done some professional guiding. But neither of us had ever experienced anything like this from other fly fishers prior to the twenty-first century. The fly fishing community has in general fostered respect for water, for fish, and for other anglers.

And this is not only true of fly fishers. We are also avid hikers, canoeists, outdoor enthusiasts in general. We are even kayakers, though admittedly my own interest is in sea kayaking rather than white water. In all of these varied activities and for most of our lives we have found members of these outdoor communities to be generally polite, helpful, respective, and congenial.

At least that was the case for a long time. Over the past few years, however, both of us have witnessed a decline in civility and a growth in rudeness. And yes, we are both getting older, but we're pretty sure this isn't merely a case of us becoming curmudgeons. The incident with the guide on the Magalloway was the most extreme we'd seen, but we have witnessed similar encounters elsewhere to lesser degrees, suggesting that the Magalloway occurrence was not an isolated event but a growing trend.

Why? One factor may be that people are fishing (and hiking and backpacking and kayaking) in more places, and as a result we are less connected to any one place. While there is an overall decline in the number of people fishing, among those who do angle there seems to be an increasing trend toward traveling in order to do that angling in famous and far-flung places. This is a simple benefit of the modern technologies of travel. In a single day of travel it is possible to get to almost any river in the United States, with the possible exception of some remote fly-in waters of Alaska. (This, it would seem, is also one of the causes of the recent spread of many invasive species such as the aforementioned didymo, which has been carried from river to river around the world on anglers' waders.) Famous trout waters in particular draw people willing to travel long distances to fish those trophy waters— and equally importantly for some, to tweet or post Facebook status updates about fishing those famous waters. We have both enjoyed fishing on many rivers around the country, and we are grateful for those opportunities. But it is easy for anglers to come to regard rivers not as connected parts of landscapes but as disconnected places, places we travel to rather than places we live in. They are not our homes, and we relax the rules of civility. The very sense of home and rootedness to a particular river disappears.

THE STRENGTH OF THE HILLS (AND RIVERS)

This problem of a lack of a sense of place, home, and belonging goes far beyond the fishing world. More than eighty years ago, C. S. Lewis and J. R. R. Tolkien were discussing the lack of rootedness in the food we eat: the lack of a sense of a home farm that supplied our meals, and the resulting lack of connectedness to a particular place. Lewis recounted this conversation to another friend.

> Tolkien once remarked to me that the feeling about home must have been quite different in the days when a family had fed on the produce of the same few miles of country for six generations, and that perhaps this was why they saw nymphs in the fountains and dryads in the wood—they were not mistaken for there was in a sense a *real* (not metaphorical) connection between them and the countryside. What had been earth and air & later corn, and later still bread, really was in them. We of course who live on a standardized international diet (you may have had Canadian flour, English meat, Scotch oatmeal, African oranges, & Australian wine to day) are really artificial beings and have no connection (save in sentiment) with any place on earth. We are synthetic men, up-rooted. The strength of the hills is not ours.[9]

We might note that in our modern world we aren't connected to water either. The strength of the mountains from which that water flows is not ours. Did you fish in Vermont today? You might have caught German brown trout, rainbow trout from the West Coast, and brook trout from Maine, while casting flies tied in Singapore and eating your snack of grapes imported from Chile.

As noted, we are among the guilty. We traveled to many rivers in many states just for our work on this book. By the end of 2012, I had caught trout in twenty-five U.S. states, three Canadian provinces, and two European countries. Though I do have my "home" rivers, I often "feast" on an international, or at least interstate, diet of trout streams. Now I try not to regard rivers as disconnected parts of landscapes. One of the goals of this book is to connect rivers to people and landscapes and stories of Appalachia, and to our own stories, and even to each other. But we must acknowledge that the disconnection is always a danger.

In addition to the loss of rootedness, another possible—though I hope not necessary—negative consequence is that an angler who has traveled hundreds of miles to fish a river like the Magalloway, and perhaps has only a day or two to fish it, may feel he or she has too much to lose by being polite. When we are fishing our local "home" rivers, and we come to a favorite hole and find another angler there, chances are it's a friend or acquaintance, and we can share greetings and stories. Even if it's somebody we don't know fishing the hole we want to fish, we know we can return the next day or the next week and fish the same spot. So we do the right thing: we move around the hole and leave the person to fish in peace. But what if we know we won't be around to return tomorrow?

There is another side to it as well. Few people want their own home to be a place of rudeness and hostility. Even if we are willing to be rude to a stranger waiting for a cab on a crowded city street, or putting an anonymous post on the Internet, we don't want that rudeness creeping into our homes. Our homes should be places of civility. Or so we hope.

But what if the river is nobody's home? What if our names are not attached to what we say and do? Then for some this motivation for civility is gone. We allow incivility to creep into the trout stream because that stream is a place that belongs to nobody; it is nobody's home. Incivility, then, is merely a symptom—a very unpleasant one, I think—of the loss of rootedness that is at least possible, if not inevitable, in a world of globetrotters. A lack of any place that is truly home is the real problem.

Is there a solution? I wonder. My instinct at the snowmobile bridge was to hold my ground—or, rather, to hold my water—and not give in to the intruders. It was easy to blame the fishing guide for his rudeness, and even to feel a certain self-righteousness in our actions. But to speak truly, our own actions did nothing to increase civility on the stream that day. Had we yielded the hole with a polite word and wishes of success to the newcomers, we might have made the river a more friendly and less competitive place that day.

Chapter 4

The Removal of Mountains, Swift and Slow

Matthew Dickerson

All waters are one. This [stream] is a reach of the sea, flung like a net over the hill, and now drawn back to the sea. And as the sea is never raised in the earthly nets of fishermen, so the hill is never caught and pulled down by the water net of the sea. But always a little of it is.

—Wendell Berry, "A Native Hill"

So there we were, on a Saturday in late May: Dave and I in Kentucky, in Cumberland Gap National Historic Park, which straddles the state's border with Virginia, ending at the corner where those two states meet Tennessee. The day was winding to a close. My legs were exhausted. I had my fly rod in hand, and I'd made plenty of casts. Hopeful casts at first. Somewhat half-hearted ones later. Half-hearted because I hadn't seen a single trout. Not only had I not gotten any strikes, I had not even been able to spook one and watch its shadow dart under a rock or log. My hopes were fading.

Some fly fishers will say their sport is not about catching fish, that bringing something into the net is not necessary to the enjoyment of angling. This is not altogether wrong, but not altogether right either. There are two important qualifications, at least for me. First, when I am angling—whether with a fly or any other way—I am always attempting and hoping to catch a fish. Catching a fish is the goal of fishing. It is the goal of choosing a fly and casting a fly. It is also what motivates my choice of where on the river to try to place that fly. There is both skill and artistry in casting a fly, and there is pleasure in the exercise of that skill in and of itself. But a big part of the pleasure of making a good cast is the pleasure of knowing that a "good cast" is the sort of cast that will catch a fish. Hooking a fish is the confirmation of the angler's casting efforts. Indeed, Dave and I often joke that hooking a fish is the best possible definition of a "good cast." A "nice cast" is one that looks good, with a tight loop that unfolds in a straight line, and lands the fly where you want it to land. A "good cast" is one that catches a fish. We prefer to make casts that are both nice and good, but given the choice between one or the other we might often choose good ones.

The other aspect of the enjoyment of fly fishing—and for me, at least, the most important one—is the aspect of hope or anticipation. As long as I have some hope of catching a fish, I enjoy every cast. I might make a hundred casts in a row without catching a fish, and enjoy every one, as long as I anticipate that each of those casts could catch a fish. That is, as long as the next cast I make might be one that lands the trout, I am having fun. Seeing fish in a river, especially watching them feed, will raise my level of anticipation. But what best keeps me hopeful that the next cast might succeed is if previous casts have been catching fish, at least occasionally. In that way, though the activity of angling is enjoyable for me even apart from the actual hooking, playing, and landing of fish, that enjoyment is bound up through anticipation and hope with the actual catching of fish.

And after fishing our way up Martin's Fork around several bends, through two or three long pools, and below some overhanging trees, that sense of the anticipation of trout was quickly waning. We were three miles deep into the woods from where we had parked our car. Given the various dead ends, false trails, and loop backs, we had probably walked closer to four miles on the way in. That didn't count our time walking up and down the stream itself. And we would have three or more miles of hiking to get out when we were done fishing. It would be at least a seven-mile day. Probably eight or nine. If part of the point of a long hike is to find trout, then that hike feels a lot longer when no trout are found. We had hiked in on unmarked trails, first wandering and backtracking around circular and S-shaped ATV trails outside the park and then eventually finding our way into the park and its trails. We finally came over a long steep ridge, and down into a deep narrow valley to a tiny historic creek known as Martin's Fork, a headwater of the Cumberland River.

Granted, it was a beautiful hike, at least once we escaped the tangle of rutted ATV trails overgrown with thorny vines. We reminded ourselves on multiple occasions that the hike itself, and our observations about the land and water, and not necessarily the fishing, were the primary purpose for our being there. The mountain laurels were already in bloom, and the wild rhododendrons—which grow to heights that would be unheard of in my home state of Vermont—were on the verge of blooming. At the bottom of the ridge where we had started, the woods and understory were thick, making it difficult to navigate even on some of the overgrown trails. But once atop the ridge, it began to look more like whitetail country. There were several species of southern oak, including both white and red varieties, plenty of browse such as wild raspberry and rhododendron, and some dense stands of fir cover.

In the background, many elusive deep-woods songbirds could be heard at times: thrushes and perhaps warblers, though I don't know bird-songs as well as I should. But they could only be heard when the cicadas fell silent. In much of Kentucky, including the Cumberland Gap, this was the seventeenth year in the cycle of a large brood of the *M. cassini* cicada: one of the cicada species with a seventeen-year cycle. In other words, it was a year for massive numbers of cicadas to emerge from the ground together and mate, creating another generation that will not be seen until this year's nursing human babies are finishing up high school.

I had never experienced a cicada hatch before, though I'd read about them. The sandy trail was covered with holes where they had emerged from the ground, as if somebody had taken a huge shotgun and aimed it at the ground from fifty feet in the air, and then just kept firing over and over again all up the trail. At times, as we moved through the woods along the ridge trail, it sounded like we were walking past a fire station with the sirens blaring at full volume. The whine of the cicadas was that loud.

It was clear that many of the gap's wild population had been feasting on the abundance of cicadas. We found fresh bear scat, loaded with cicada wings. In another spot, the clear scratch marks of a turkey could be seen amongst a litter of cicada holes. And shortly after spotting the scratching, we heard a turkey crashing through the brush just off the trail. If even a fraction of these cicadas fell into the water, any trout living nearby would have a feast that summer.

The woods were also full of ticks. I was wearing Insect Shield attire: socks, pants, and a shirt whose fabric was manufacturer-treated with the tick and mosquito repellent Permethrin. Dave was wearing pants he had treated himself with spray. Within a mile he was regularly finding ticks on his clothing and pulling them off. At least half a dozen found their way onto him. I didn't get any on me. Dave claimed it was our body chemistry, not the clothing. Either way, the number of ticks was creepy and I would be double-checking behind my ears and along the hairline on the back of my neck for days.

One thing we didn't find in Martin's Fork, however, were wild brook trout. We had been sent there by both a state fisheries biologist and a professional forester named Hagan Wonn. Hagan also works two days a week as a professional fishing guide on the Cumberland River, and we would meet him early the next morning for a guided day of fishing from a drift boat on the famous tailwater stretch of the Cumberland many miles downriver below the reservoir. To be clear, neither the biologist nor the guide-forester offered any claim that we would find what we were looking for. They simply *suggested* that it was a *possibility* that we *might* find some remnant population of brookies here, because the area was now so remote and undeveloped. The stream had, years before, been stocked with brook trout, they said. Probably somewhere down below the park. Whether the trout had made their way upstream or not, whether they had survived and established a self-sustaining breeding population, whether the stream was even capable of holding a self-sustaining population of wild brook trout, neither of the men knew. We were interested in finding out.

What we did discover is that Martin's Fork is tiny near its source up in the Cumberland Gap National Historic Park. It is even smaller than we imagined. And the air even in late May—before the official start of summer—was hot. The question was whether, down at the bottom of a deep and steep cut, with a thick canopy over the stream, this headwater of the Cumberland could stay cool enough for trout. Our observations suggested the answer was yes. We found plenty of shaded pools up to three feet deep, mixed with some cascades and riffs, and it felt cool enough on our feet. We tested the pH at about 5.4, which is acidic, but not outside the tolerable range for brook trout. And the water proved rich in life. The first stone we overturned in the stream revealed a half dozen tiny crayfish, some small salamanders, and a caddis fly casing with a live caddis nymph. All good trout food. We soon spotted three different mayfly species flying over the water—even more good food, and also a promising sign of healthy water.

From where the trail crossed the water, we bushwhacked and waded and fished our way about a half a mile up the creek. Further upstream we found even more crayfish, including some whoppers. These were crayfish big enough that we could imagine them eating small trout, rather than becoming food for them. These were crayfish that made us step quickly out of the water.

Crayfish, though, were not what we wanted. We were looking for evidence of wild brook trout, and for indications of the health, or lack thereof, of the stream ecosystems. We knew, of course, that any wild trout we might find were not of direct descent from an indigenous strain. If any were there at all, they would be the results of stocking efforts some time in the past few years or decades, not fish whose ancestors had inhabited this stretch of water for centuries. Even if by miracle indigenous brook trout had survived coal mining, mountaintop removal, and deforestation in some small highland stream somewhere else in Kentucky, it was astronomically unlikely they had survived here. The ridge, though now once again well forested, had been completely cleared of trees in the nineteenth century to offer a better view for the artillery placed on top of the ridge to guard the famed Wilderness Road that runs along its southern side. Still, we wanted to find some headwater of the Cumberland that might once again be holding trout. It would be a sign of hope.

MAKING MOLEHILLS OUT OF MOUNTAINS

The path that brought us here was winding in both a metaphorical and literal sense. In the early evening of the previous day we pulled off the road in a small and very rural eastern Tennessee town and into the gravel parking lot of some closed local store in order to study a map. Several long days of fishing, with many miles of wading, had taken a toll on Dave's wading shoes. The felt sole on one was falling off. Finding a replacement set of felt soles out in the middle of nowhere seemed unlikely. But perhaps we might find a small hardware store selling duct tape. Duct tape, as we all know, can fix anything. We were wondering what nearby town was most likely to have duct tape.

It turns out the appearance in his town of strangers with an out-of-state license—we had a rental car from further south, in North Carolina, but with plates from the northern state of Ohio—caught the attention of the local sheriff, who had begun to follow us through town. When we pulled off, he pulled into the parking lot beside us, perhaps to see what we were up to, or perhaps just to let us know that he was watching. Scenes from the movie *Deliverance* popped into my mind. Dave, the son of a deputy sheriff in New York, must have had the same fears that had suddenly leapt to my mind. But he was thinking faster than I was. Before the sheriff could approach our car and grill us about why we were driving around his town with out-of-state plates, Dave jumped out of our car and approached him—eagerly, but not too threateningly. I followed more reluctantly. "Boy, are we glad to see you," Dave said, hoping to make it clear we had nothing to hide.

The conversation that followed—if it can be called a conversation—still boggles me, in large part because I have no idea what we were talking about. The sheriff spoke to Dave. We could not understand a word he said. In fact, we wondered how anybody could understand him. He acted friendly enough, but he had an East Tennessee accent as thick as overcooked grits. He rambled on about something or other, and then stopped as though he had satisfactorily explained himself. Not having any idea what he said, we just smiled and nodded. Dave then explained that we were looking for a hardware store to buy some supplies. The sheriff paused a moment, and then said something else that was, again, completely unintelligible to us. It wasn't that there were a few words here and there that we could not make out. We could not make out a single word of what he said. He made a few motions with his hands. The only word or phrase we could later remember was something that sounded like "wahlawhorl," drawn out nice and long but simultaneously with the syllables all slurred together. We remembered this word because after he said it he gave a belly laugh as though he'd told a really good joke. We did not want to appear unappreciative and get ourselves arrested for being from out of town, or worse yet, out of state, so again we smiled and nodded and thanked him profusely for his sage advice. We might even have made an attempt to laugh, since it seemed as though we were expected to. If I conjured up a laugh, though, it was a hollow one. The sheriff said something else that was completely lost on us. We smiled, thanked him for his local knowledge and helpful words, returned to our car, and drove off, making an effort to conform our driving to the sheriff's hand gestures, since we hadn't understood his words.

The effort paid off. Eventually we found a Walmart in a much larger town about twenty miles away, where we also stopped for dinner at a local restaurant. We later decided that "wahlawhorl" had probably meant "Wally World," which in turn was slang for Walmart. Walmart not only had duct tape, but in their fishing section they actually had a felt replacement kit for wading shoes. That night in a small hotel in a Virginia town near the edge of the Cumberland Gap, we repaired Dave's shoes. And so, despite the language barrier, the congenial sheriff's generosity in taking the time to help strangers really did prove helpful. Maybe he was a fisherman himself, and when we identified ourselves as fishermen he saw us as kindred spirits and took a liking to us. Or maybe he also had no idea what we were saying in our thick Yankee accents, and months later he still tells stories about the incomprehensible foreigners who stopped in his town one afternoon.

One guidebook on fly fishing for trout in the southern Appalachians makes reference to the dangers anglers face when fishing mountain trout streams. The author suggests that—although he had met folks who had unreasoned fears to the contrary—neither rattlesnakes nor black bears posed any significant danger to anglers fishing small mountain streams. Neither did water moccasins. We could now attest, despite our own initial fears, that getting harassed or arrested by a small-town cop for being strangers didn't turn out to be a real danger either in that small town in eastern Tennessee on that particular day. (I suppose the bigger danger was getting lost while trying assiduously to follow directions we could not understand.) In any case, the author of that guidebook said the greatest danger was slipping on a wet rock and plunging over a waterfall.

On the other hand, while the local sheriff had proved congenial and in a way helpful, and not at all threatening, we had heard serious accounts from professional guides, wardens, and foresters of clans up in the mountains who had replaced the old moonshine trade with a much more sophisticated and profitable trade in marijuana, grown on public land in the national parks and forests. In order to minimize the chances of getting caught in the act of cultivation, they would visit their marijuana groves only a couple times of year. The rest of the year they protected their investments with mantraps: booby traps of one sort or another designed to maim or kill nosy intruders. We were told of monofilament fishing line, nearly invisible, strung with tiny hooks at eye level across ATV paths, of tripwires rigged to makeshift shotguns aimed at knee level across footpaths, and even of tripwires connected to cans of soda. This last one bewildered us until it was explained that a can of soda attracts hornets, and anyone tipping the can over would be stung mercilessly. It may be that the primary purpose of these were to keep people, including rival growers, from stealing an expensive crop. But the booby traps were likewise dangerous to law enforcement officers and anglers. These mountain drug growers, we were told, shot strangers on sight. More than one of the otherwise bold and brave outdoor professionals who told us these stories lived with a fear of being out in the woods one day and stumbling into one of these marijuana groves, and never returning.

We spend enough time in the woods to know that sometimes in the middle of nowhere you run into things that have been put there by people who don't want them to be found. It's not always marijuana. When pheasant hunting in South Dakota, Dave avoids old outbuildings on abandoned farms because they are often found and used—and ruthlessly defended—as meth labs. During one of our excursions in the southern Appalachians, Dave and I had stumbled upon a few old barrels half buried under tarps and brush. We had imagined it part of some illicit operation, and it had unnerved us some.

As we drove down the back roads of the rural southeastern corner of Kentucky the next morning, working our way to the hiking trails leading into the Cumberland Gap, those fears arose once more. We did not get the impression that the few houses we passed would be welcoming to strangers. Whether the danger was real or imagined, we did not give in to our fears but pressed on. We had a question we wanted to ask.

The same guidebook that discussed the dangers of bears, snakes, and slick rocks also makes mention of indigenous brook trout in Kentucky, stating that "the only trout naturally occurring in the Blue Grass State were probably found in the thin ribbon of the Blue Ridge Mountains located in the extreme eastern rim of the state."[10] The author goes on to mention an effort at the "experimental reintroduction of native southern Appalachian brook trout" and the fact that "fisheries managers of the state are rather reluctant to identify the creeks." This author admits that the native presence of wild brook trout in Kentucky may have been minimal compared with that of other more mountainous Appalachian states. But he still does not question that the trout did at one time exist, before the deforestation wrought by European settlers wiped them out. Then later stocking efforts of other Europeans brought the brook trout back—along with rainbow trout and brown trout. But what evidence did he have for that conclusion for a book first published in 1994? Writing in the late twentieth century, did he have a way of knowing where brook trout had lived two centuries earlier? Or was he just guessing, relying on a mix of common sense, geography, and the current ecological conditions of Kentucky streams? His use of the word *probably* indicates uncertainty. That uncertainty could go in either direction. It could apply to his guess that the range was never very extensive; perhaps it had been more extensive than he imagined. But the uncertainty might also be just a guess that the state held indigenous trout at all; perhaps it hadn't.

And why would fisheries biologists be reluctant to identify the creeks in which reintroduction efforts are happening? Is it to protect those waters from overzealous anglers? Or is it to avoid acknowledging that such an effort is based on the fact that the brook trout existed there in the first place, before Europeans came and settled the state?

Whatever reasons the author of the aforementioned guidebook may have had to claim the pre-European existence of trout in Kentucky, Dave, in his research, found a much older source suggesting such a claim is justified—that Kentucky did have indigenous brook trout. In a book titled *The Speckled Brook Trout*, published in 1902, the editor makes the following claim:

> Trout of some sort are found in the six New England states, New York, New Jersey, Pennsylvania, Maryland, Virginia, West Virginia, North Carolina, South Carolina, Georgia, Tennessee, Kentucky, *Ohio*, *Indiana*, Michigan, Wisconsin, Minnesota, Iowa, *Missouri*, *Arkansas*, New Mexico, Colorado, *Nebraska*, *South Dakota*, *North Dakota*, Montana, Wyoming, Idaho, Washington, Oregon, California, Chihuahua, Texas and Alaska. It is not native to any of those italicized, and is found in very limited portions only of New Jersey, Maryland, South Carolina, Georgia, Tennessee, Kentucky, and Texas.[11]

The editor, though acknowledging that trout were found only in "very limited portions" of Kentucky, still include Kentucky among the states where trout could be found, and furthermore claim that it is native in the states not italicized—which includes Kentucky. If any native trout existed in Kentucky, they were certainly brook trout; only brook trout and their kin, the char, are indigenous to the Appalachians. Of course, this is by no means conclusive evidence of native brook trout in Kentucky. Still, the authors of that 1902 book were obviously aware of trout existing in Kentucky, and it seems very reasonable they would have known whether those fish were native, as European brown trout (the popularly stocked trout in the nineteenth century) were not native anywhere in North America.

So why did this matter? And how did it end up driving us to spend a day tromping around the Cumberland Gap three miles deep in the woods with fly rods? When I fish a trout stream with a good canopy, I am thankful that the water is cooler, protected from the sun. I may at times silently curse the branch that snags my fly midair or prevents me from making a cast that will reach a certain hole before my shadow falls across it. But I know the canopy gives trout a better chance of survival in the hot summer months. It keeps them feeding longer into the morning on days I am out casting for them. It also protects the river from erosion, and slows the rate at which fertilizers and pesticides become part of the rivers and lakes. It prevents the eggs of fish and the larvae of insects from being buried in silt. I appreciate the farmers, loggers and foresters, landowners, and others who leave—or even make the effort to create—sound riparian buffers.

Poet, essayist, novelist, and Kentucky native Wendell Berry, in his essay "A Native Hill," describes the slow but inexorable shaping of the land around his home by the waters of the local creek as it makes its way down to its home at sea level. "We are a long way from the coast, and the sea is alien to us," he writes. "And yet the attraction of sea level dwells in this country as an idea dwells in a man's mind. All our rains go in search of it and, departing, they have carved the land in a shape that is fluent and falling." A little later he elaborates.

> All waters are one. This [stream] is a reach of the sea, flung like a net over the hill, and now drawn back to the sea. And as the sea is never raised in the earthly nets of fishermen, so the hill is never caught and pulled down by the water net of the sea. But always a little of it is. Each of the gathering strands of the net carries back some of the hill melted in it. Sometimes, as now, it carries so little that the water flows clear; sometimes it carries a lot and is brown and heavy with it. Whenever greedy or thoughtless men have lived on it, the hill has literally flowed out of their tracks into the bottom of the sea.[12]

This reality of slow erosion is a story told continually on every stream on earth. When I stand in a trout stream, fly rod in hand, looking at off-colored water, I am assessing the level of murkiness and whether it will help or hinder the fishing. Will fish be feeding at all? If so, what fly is appropriate for the conditions? But I know also that what I am looking at in that off-colored water is the mountain making its way to the ocean.

The process is, as I said, inexorable. It would happen whether humans dwelt on the land or not. But our species does have a habit of accelerating that process, by our building of roads, our felling of trees, the grazing of grasses by our domesticated animals, and our tilling of soil. The use of more careful practices in lumbering, tilling, road building, and grazing may minimize this impact. Less careful practices, while perhaps more economical and efficient—better, perhaps, for short-term profit—pay little heed to the impact. This reality hit home for me in the summer of 2012 when Tropical Storm Irene swept across Vermont with its devastating power. I remember many images of both roads and farm fields in the mountains where entire swaths of soil, some five feet deep, ten yards wide, a hundred yards long, simply disappeared into trout streams I have often fished, swept away by the torrent to end up in Lake Champlain or the Connecticut River.

And that devastation witnessed in town after town across Vermont is nothing compared to the destruction caused by the coal-mining technique known as mountaintop removal. Mountaintop removal is now the predominant method of coal mining in Kentucky, West Virginia, and throughout the Appalachians. As its names suggests, the process involves the complete removal of entire mountains. All of the trees, soil, rock, and other material above a vein of coal, collectively (and disparagingly) called an "overburden," must be taken away by explosives and giant earthmoving equipment. This overburden can be as thick as four hundred feet. More than one thousand metric tons of explosives are used per day in Kentucky for mountaintop removal. By the early part of this decade, 2,200 square miles of Appalachian forests had been cleared for mountaintop removal, with over 1.4 million acres of mountain top removed—an area larger than the state of Delaware.

That is a tremendous scale of destruction, and a tremendous volume of material. Of course, it must be dumped some place. That place too often is a neighboring valley, or a stream that then ceases to be a stream. It is difficult or impossible for me to think of the healthy trees and soils of an Appalachian mountain as a burden. But when they are removed from the mountain and dumped into a nearby river valley, mixed with rock and often with the toxic by-products of mining, it becomes a burden indeed, one placed on the shoulders of the river and all the creatures—great and small—that depend upon it. Thus the area of devastation far exceeds the area of the mountain and the mine itself.

According to a 2003 Environmental Protection Agency report, more than twelve hundred miles of headwater stream had been "directly impacted" by mountaintop removal in the decade from 1992 to 2002. Here, perhaps, the word *impacted* does not communicate clearly enough how significant the damage to rivers had been. Estimates are that in just the decade and a half from 1985 to 2001 over seven hundred miles of river—enough to reach from the northern border of Vermont down to the southern border, and back again—simply disappeared, completely buried beneath mountain debris called "valley fills."[13] How many thousands or tens of thousands of fish? How many hundreds of thousands of mayflies, caddis flies, stone flies? How many birds that live in those forests and eat those trout and insects? And that report was already a decade old. How much more has happened since?

It is true that everything lives downstream. Simply removing the stream doesn't change that metaphoric fact. Another report studied the effect of mountaintop removal on the downstream portions of rivers and creeks that were not buried. In Appalachian streams that are healthy and unimpacted by mountaintop removal, the family of insects known as *Ephemeroptera*—that is, mayflies—are in general a major component of the macroinvertebrate aquatic life. One report says that "they account for 25 to 50% of total macroinvertebrate abundance in least-disturbed Central Appalachian streams sampled in the spring." The finding of that study is that "entire orders of benthic organisms (e.g., Ephemeroptera) were nearly eliminated in [mountaintop removal]." The conclusion that this "is a cause for concern and is evidence that the aquatic life use is being impaired" is an understatement.[14]

But mountaintop removal does provide coal. Its concern is not to ask, What is the purpose of the mountain and how can we honor that purpose? Nor does it ask about the purpose of the trees, birds, insects, and animals that live on the mountain or the rivers that flow off of them. Perhaps in the past it was simple to say what the purpose of something like a mountain is. What a mountain is. What a mountain is for. What it means. Or maybe that's just false nostalgia. In any case, we find it hard in our time to agree on what mountains are for. Which usually means that the people with the money get to decide what they're for. And that, it seems to me, is a shame. Instead of asking what a mountain is for, mountaintop removal asks, How can we provide coal for which there is a market, and how can we provide it most efficiently? For the burning of coal provides energy to power our lights and computers and microwave ovens and cell phones and cell towers. All the things we cannot live without. And so there is an economy in the removal of mountains. It makes money for the shareholders of the coal companies that do the removing. And because there is an economic side to mountaintop removal, there is also a political side.

I freely admit that I do not know the extent to which politics plays a role in historical or scientific studies, or even in fisheries policies. But there is much here that I find curious. Kentucky and neighboring West Virginia are the states where mountaintop removal is most commonly practiced. The state fisheries biologists we interviewed from Kentucky denied that brook trout were ever a native species in the state. They deny that *S. fontinalis* could be found in its waters prior to the arrival of Europeans on what is now Kentucky soil, and prior to their stocking efforts in what are now Kentucky rivers and streams. More than a mere denial, the state biologists seemed bothered that we would ask the question. *Reluctant* was the word another author used to describe the unwillingness of fisheries managers in Kentucky to respond to questions about wild brook trout streams. The words *suspicious* and *uneasy* better describe what I sensed. It may be that science really did convince these biologists that brook trout were not indigenous in the state, and they didn't like people suggesting otherwise. It may also be that, for political reasons, they were given an official position they were required to hold to, and yet were uneasy with that position. It might just be they were suspicious of my motives in asking. I do not know, and didn't have a good way of finding out.

Whatever the case, their denial is stunning. Brook trout were ubiquitous up and down the length of the Appalachians from Georgia to Maine. And thanks to efforts of state and national fisheries biologists, the National Park Service, and groups like the Eastern Joint Brook Trout Venture, they are being found in these waters once again. They once again inhabit the headwaters of the Holston River not very far from Martin's Fork and the headwaters of the Cumberland. They can be found across the border from Kentucky eastward in West Virginia and Virginia, and south in Tennessee. Is it possible that brook trout really did not exist in Kentucky prior to stocking?

Now I admit an emotional bias here. I would like to think that the indigenous peoples of Kentucky honored the red and yellow and black speckles on the beautiful dark mottled backs of the char before Europeans cut the trees off the mountains of eastern Kentucky and destroyed the habitat that might have supported wild brook trout. Why do I privilege the brook trout? Why do I want to think that brook trout used to live in Kentucky? Walleye are another fish that thrive in cold, clean waters. In Kentucky, walleye and not brook trout may be the best indicator of a healthy river and a healthy ecosystem. They are certainly indigenous to the colder waters of Kentucky, and to much larger portions of the state than brook trout ever were. If we were writing this book about Kentucky alone, and wanted to explore a fish of historical, cultural, and ecological health in the Appalachian highlands of the eastern part of the state, we should probably focus on the walleye.

And there are indeed reasons why one might doubt the presence of wild brook trout in Kentucky. As the guidebook *Trout Streams of Southern Appalachia* states, the part of Kentucky where the habitat is (and was) suitable to brook trout is only a narrow ribbon of land in the Blue Ridge Mountains in the eastern part of the state. Most of the rest of the state simply lacks the higher altitudes necessary for brook trout in a state so far south. The ribbon of land is not empty, of course. It still contains thousands of acres and hundreds of miles of streams. Still, despite how widespread brook trout were in the rest of Appalachia three centuries ago, it is conceivable that brook trout somehow never made it to Kentucky when they managed to migrate to every other Appalachian state. Perhaps even the 1902 book on brook trout was wrong. We have not yet found any earlier written sources mentioning the presence of indigenous brookies in Kentucky. And if there were any brook trout, deforestation almost certainly wiped them out decades ago. Any indigenous population would likely be gone by now, unless it was reintroduced.

That, however, is a very different thing from denying they ever existed. And here, as I noted, is where I can't help wondering what role politics plays. For if Kentucky really did have indigenous brook trout, and if some of the streams of eastern Kentucky are now supporting wild populations of a fish that really is a native fish—even if the actual existing population has in its ancestry some imported strain—there might be negative ramifications to the multibillion dollar coal industry and its practice of mountaintop removal. Mining, including not only the removal of material but the filling of nearby valleys and the discharging of pollutants into streams, is all regulated under the Clean Water Act. To cite again from the published scientific study on the downstream effects of mountaintop coal mining, the Clean Water Act "directs states and tribes to designate beneficial uses for streams." And, as should be the case, "most waters in the US are designated for 'aquatic life uses,' which means the water must support fish, shellfish, insects, and other wildlife that inhabit the water." Referring to the 2007 narrative of the "Water Quality Standard for the Department of Environmental Protection" for the state of Kentucky, the wording is even more important. "Total dissolved solids or specific conductance [resulting from mining] shall not be changed to the extent that the indigenous aquatic community is adversely affected."[15]

There can be no question that mountaintop removal destroys local streams. And, of course, any population of fish they might hold are, to understate the case, "adversely affected," along with the other life in the stream such as the aquatic invertebrates. Here the word *indigenous* becomes important. The presence of a rare indigenous fish in those streams—say a wild brook trout, a fish that needed to be protected—might give just a piece of ammunition to those opposed to mountaintop removal on ecological grounds. And while one might argue that walleye are widely enough distributed around the entire state that they need not be protected in one particular stream, the ribbon of land where indigenous brook trout may have lived in Kentucky would need to be protected. The question of whether brook trout are indigenous to Kentucky is not just an academic one then. It would be nice if brook trout could be found again, restored—and if their presence could prevent even just one mountaintop from being removed.

IN PURSUIT OF KENTUCKY TROUT:
SALVATION IN A TAIL

When Dave and I arrived back at the car at the end of the afternoon after our day in the Cumberland Gap, we had no evidence that any brook trout were currently present in Martin's Fork. On our drive out of the Gap, we stopped at one other stream: Shilalah Creek. Shilalah is another of the small headwater tributaries of the Cumberland. It is a prettier stream than Martin's Fork. It cascades among a tumble of massive boulders through a forest of hardwoods down the steep northwestern slope of the Cumberland Gap ridgeline. It looks more trouty, with its falls and plunge pools and clear water. And the temperature and fragrance of the air were very pleasant as we walked under the shade of a high canopy of oak leaves. Yet Shillalah Creek, like Martin's Fork, did not offer us any evidence of brook trout. On this venture, we had failed.

The day in the Cumberland Gap on the Martin's Fork and Shillalah Creek were not my first failed fishing ventures in Kentucky. A couple of years earlier I was in the Lexington area visiting the editor of a series of books that would soon be including one of my titles. Hoping to go fishing on my one free afternoon, I searched for possible trout waters within driving distance. A few sources suggested that the short tailwater stretch of the Dix River below Herrington Dam as it runs through a narrow canyon down to its confluence with the Kentucky River was the nearest trout stream to Lexington. So I bought a one-day fishing license and drove down to the Dix in my rental car. I then spent two hours driving all the way up and down both sides of the canyon—and discovered not a single public access to the river. Unless one is a landowner on the river, the only way to fish the Dix is to put in a canoe at a public landing on the Kentucky River and paddle all the way up from below. For the only time in my life, I bought a one-day license and didn't even wet a fly, though not for a lack of trying.

Haunted by my failure, I managed to return the following year on another trip to visit the same editor and to give a talk at Georgetown College, just north of Lexington. The difference on this second trip was that, after reading a fishing column I wrote for the local paper about my failures on the first trip, a friend immediately contacted me and said she had a friend who lived on the Dix River! The world grows smaller all the time. And so, thanks to a friend of a friend, I not only had private access to the river but a canoe to borrow. My brother Ted, his wife Susie, and my nephews Brad and Michael drove up from North Carolina and met me for the weekend. While Susie unloaded her easel and oils for a day of riverside sketching and painting, the rest of us paddled up the river from our access point to a ledge and section of riffles below the dam where we could wade. We enjoyed a very pleasant day casting flies. I don't remember what flies I used. I do remember that I caught several brown trout and erased the earlier failure. Likewise, I hope one day to find some headwater of the Cumberland holding wild brook trout. Maybe by then we will have better evidence that the species was once indigenous.

Meanwhile, though, the Cumberland River did redeem itself in one way. The tailwater of the Cumberland below the dam on Cumberland Lake bears about as much resemblance to Martin's Fork as a #6 cone-head wooly bugger does to a #18 blue-wing olive. It is not, by any stretch of the imagination, an Appalachian river. It left the mountains many miles upstream. All that remains of Appalachia is the water itself. What the Cumberland tailwater is is a trophy trout water. The most famous in Kentucky. And justifiably so.

Our guide, Hagan Wonn, meets Dave and me at 5:30 a.m. at our little cabin rental. It is his day off from his private forestry business, and a day for him to guide instead. Most guides and anglers on the Cumberland work from motorboats. Behind his big pickup Hagan is towing a Montana-style drift boat. His university training in forestry came in Montana, and while fishing the rivers out west he fell in love with the drift boat. He claims to be the only guide on the Cumberland to use one regularly, and our observations of other anglers on that day bear this up. Hagan's knowledge of forestry is also evident, and we appreciate the abundant information he shares about the local plants and animals. His knowledge of the fauna is much broader than merely his knowledge of the trout in the river—though that is certainly more than sufficient. He also has answers to most of our questions about the local flora, and he doesn't consider trees and flowers merely in relation to the trout. He is interested in ecology in the broad sense of that word.

We are on the river below the dam by 6:30 a.m. and casting flies not too long after that. The morning is misty and damp. Though the massive and towering thunderheads that filled the sky with pink the previous evening are gone, we are wearing raincoats.

The river is deep and swift, and we realize it would be next to impossible to wade. With the exception of a few rocky outcroppings, fly casting from the steep, wooded shoreline would also be a great challenge, if not impossible. The drift boat, however, is perfect. It gives access to the whole river. And Hagan knows the river well. The water is clear and clean with a pale green tint. It is also tailwater cold, and quite swift. Hagan comments that we wouldn't survive long if we fell in. This may sound ominous for humans, but it is promising for those seeking trout. Fish food is also abundant. All around us, coming from the woods on every side, echoing across the slopes on both sides of the river, we hear the continual whine of a hundred thousand cicadas. Soon they will start flying, and when they do they will land on the water by the thousands, providing a lot of meals to Cumberland trout. Dave and I consider how much fun we would have being on the water when that happened.

Not that we won't have fun today. Before we even land our first fish, we have a good bit of adrenaline-charged excitement. A short distance downstream from the boat ramp where we put in, an explosion in the water downstream from our boat draws our attention. A massive fish, twelve, fifteen, or even eighteen pounds, is thrashing in the shallows. Wide-eyed, we look at Hagan. "Striped bass," he tells us.

It takes a moment for that to register. Striped bass are an ocean fish, found mostly in the Atlantic along the northern half of the eastern United States. They are a great game fish. I have caught them fly casting off the coast of Maine while fishing in flats. But they can adapt to freshwater life. Even those living in saltwater will often swim up freshwater rivers chasing baitfish. They have been stocked in many freshwater lakes, including some impoundments on the Cumberland downstream of the tailwater. They swim up the river and feast on the rainbow trout that are heavily stocked in the Cumberland. Presumably, a rainbow trout was meeting its fate at that moment. We consider tying on a big streamer and going after the striper. But when we see the fish, it is still three or four times as far away as either of us can cast. It is gone before we can reach it. It would have been too much for our 5-wt rods anyway. We settle for rainbows.

And we make a good day of them. Though we do have some success on olive wooly buggers, we spend most of the day casting small nymphs on 6x tippet below strike indicators. We also spend most of the day hooking, landing, and releasing fat and healthy rainbow trout in a swift current. Most of the fish are sixteen to seventeen inches long, though some are bigger. Their size, the lightness of our tippets, and the swift current combine to turn many battles into three- or four-minute affairs.

We also miss a few fish. By late morning, Dave has caught enough trout to be satisfied and his attention wanders to the local landscape. He asks Hagan more questions about trees. Hagan answers them. The forester's background comes out. He can give us common names or scientific names of most of the species around us. Looking up at the trees, Dave misses more than one strike from a fish. Hagan grows impatient with this. "Set the hook," he snaps when Dave's strike indicator bobs below the surface. A moment later, which is also a moment too late, Dave absent-mindedly lifts his rod to hook some air. "You just missed a strike," Hagan says with disgust. So we pay more attention and land more fish. The casting and landing of many big fish takes its toll on our arms and shoulders.

After Dave lands a particularly fat rainbow on light 6x tippet—a trout running nineteen inches that gives him a fight for a quarter of an hour—I see him dangling his sore and tired arms at his side. Having caught three fish that size myself in just one particularly productive short stretch of river, I can sympathize. The day is winding to a close, and my arms are exhausted. The only thing the day has had in common with the previous one is that I hadn't seen a single trout . . . under twelve inches.

By the time we pull off the river Dave and I have landed at least fifty brown and rainbow trout between us. They're not natives, of course. They had been, and continue to be, stocked. Still, they are big and muscular. The water is clean and cold. It is seemingly unaffected here by mountaintop removal. But we know, even here, we are downstream. In bits and pieces, tiny fragments, the mountains of Kentucky are beneath our feet.

Fourth Dam

Knowing and *Knowing*

David O'Hara

Lack of experience diminishes our power of taking a comprehensive view of the admitted facts. Hence those who dwell in intimate association with nature and its phenomena grow more and more able to formulate, as the foundations of their theories, principles such as to admit of a wide and coherent development: while those whom devotion to abstract discussions has rendered unobservant of the facts are too ready to dogmatize on the basis of a few observations.

—ARISTOTLE[16]

SEVERAL YEARS AGO, I was fishing in a lake in Ontario. I paddled a kayak and trolled a lure behind me. I had been out on the deep water, hoping for a lake trout. Now, as I came back to our cottage on a narrow channel, I continued to let my lure drift behind the boat. My son Matthew, who was ten at the time, stood on the shore as I slowly paddled by, and asked me why I was fishing when we didn't need any fish for food. I have to admit that his question gave me pause, and for a moment I felt quite uncertain. As parents often do, I started speaking before I knew what I was going to say. I told him that there are a number of reasons—which is true, though I'm not sure I can put all of them into words—but that one significant reason for me is that fishing is a kind of searching, a kind of census-taking that shows me what is alive in the water below me.[17] As I look back on it, my answer to Matthew's question strikes me as both true and not entirely satisfying. I can justify catching fish when I need them as food to sustain my own life, but let's admit it: in America today we can reasonably anticipate getting all the food we need from a grocery store, without having to directly cause any animals to suffer. Can I justify catching fish and causing them to suffer when I do not mean to eat them? Some people will argue that the pain that a fish experiences is not real, or that it is not like human pain, or that the part of the fish that is hooked (the very thin skin near the jaw) has fewer nerves than other parts of its body. Others have argued that the distress that a fish appears to undergo is not like human distress because a fish lacks the capacity to experience and process emotional or psychological trauma the way that humans can. Fish memories are supposed to be short, so their suffering is brief and quickly forgotten.

I suppose there is some truth in all of that, but I don't entirely buy it. When I feel a fish on my line, I know that fish is trying to get off the line, and that it is willing to expend all its energy trying to do so. Many fish will fight until they die of exhaustion if you allow them to do so. When I hook a fish, is it in pain? Does it understand or experience pain as I do? Will its mind or its soul be scarred by this experience? I don't know, but I do know that the fish does not seem to like what is happening to it, and that it is trying to get away and make it stop.

Fly-fishers are among the fishers most willing to admit all this, perhaps because we feel a certain (but dubious) superiority to all other fishers with the possible exception of subsistence fishers. (I emphasize this word *possible*; some fly fishers would say that the fact that they do not kill fish makes them superior even to subsistence fishers. Let us leave that aside for now.) We feel superior because a trout caught by a reasonably good fly fisher has a very good chance of survival, whereas fish caught and released by bait-fishers or other lure-fishers have considerably higher mortality rates. Bait-fishers often allow fish to swallow barbed hooks, causing internal damage to the fish when they're hooked, even more damage as they're hauled in, and further damage when the hook is disgorged. This often requires rough handling of the fish, further reducing the fish's chances if it is to be released. The fly fisher, by contrast, usually uses a small, single, barbless hook that catches the fish on the jaw or lip. The fly fisher's ethic calls for the fish to be brought in quickly so as not to exhaust it; for it to be handled with wet hands (to protect its thin protective layer of mucus) and a gentle touch (to protect its internal organs) if it is to be touched at all; for it not to be held long out of the water, if at all; and for it to be released quickly if it is not to be killed.

So we admit all this but we know it does not justify what we do; it only says that we do less harm than others. This is not a defense but a diversion of attention: if you don't like what I'm doing, then you should go complain to that other fellow who's doing it twice as much. Deal with him, if you like, since he's the major offender; I'm small potatoes compared with him. And while you do that, I'll go back to fishing, having distracted you for a while.

You may ask, "If you know that you're doing some harm and you're doing it in an activity that you do not need to engage in, why do it at all?" This is becoming an easier and easier question for Americans to ask because each year fewer and fewer of us are fishing. Every state reports a steady decline in the number of fishing and hunting licenses sold over the last forty years, even as populations in most states have increased. We are, as a nation, less and less interested in hunting and fishing. We are becoming a nation of what sociologist Patricia Zaradic calls "videophiles," who spend our lives indoors, our experiences mediated by screens. It is enough for us to have virtual experiences. We are modern-day Gnostics who scorn the life of the body in favor of the imaginary life, the life of images on our glowing screens. The fact is, we all cause harm to other living things in order to continue to live. No doubt, much of this is accidental, as when trucks delivering produce to markets kill animals on the road. Even vegetarians are not exempt from this, as most farms—even organic farms—find themselves needing to kill pests that eat or uproot produce in the fields. Farming may seem a bloodless activity, but I imagine that is not the worm's perspective, nor the perspective of the many birds, rodents, and lagomorphs that make the fields their winter homes. As Tovar Cerulli has argued in his book *The Mindful Carnivore*, we all cause animal suffering and death. Obviously, some people choose not to eat meat in order to minimize this suffering. Many others put the suffering out of mind by not living near it or not participating in it.

But there is another way to approach this problem. I fish, in part, to live differently. Aldo Leopold, in his classic *A Sand County Almanac*, writes that "there are two spiritual dangers in not owning a farm." These are that if we do not farm, we do not know where our food and our fuel come from. One could reply that of course we know that our food comes from other people's farms, and that our fuel comes from petroleum or wind or hydroelectric or something like that. If we're reasonably well educated, we may even be able to explain in some detail where our food and fuel come from, and how they come to us. Leopold knows this, of course, but that is not what he means by "knowing." There is the kind of knowing that comes from reading about a thing or seeing it on a screen, and then there is the kind of knowing that comes from actually doing a thing. If you think about what we mean when we refer, with a wink, to "knowing in the *biblical* sense," you will see what I mean. It is one thing to know about a person we love; it is quite another to, well, *know* that person.

Why should it be any different with nature, and with the very food we eat? Leopold, who was not, as near as I can tell, a religious man, nevertheless calls this ignorance a "spiritual danger." When all our food comes from the grocery, we are effectively saying that the production of our food is something we are content to know about in a merely abstract way. When we eat meat, we let others mediate the death and suffering for us. We gladly distance ourselves from this gory reality, but why, and at what cost? When we do so, are we not in danger of saying that some of the most vital activities we engage in—producing and procuring the nourishment we take in—are not important enough for us to have living familiarity with them? This is what Leopold means when he calls this a spiritual danger.

One of my friends, a dairy farmer, likes to tell about a couple from New York City who came to visit his farm in Vermont. They said they loved the place, and that maybe they, too, would like to run a dairy farm—after they retired. Not having lived on a dairy farm, they had no idea just how much work it is to run one; the farm they visited was a pretty bit of scenery, a bauble one could dream of owning, not a place of hard work. Farmers traditionally have no patience for nonfarmers romanticizing farm life, and neither did Leopold. Harvesting our own vegetables and meat is not light work, and it entails both toil and risk. And arguably, as people leave the country and move to the city, it's much harder for everyone to be engaged in the production of some of their own food. So why should we privilege and pay such attention to this one vital activity of food production over other vital activities that city dwellers may more easily focus on?

I cannot answer for all people; all I can say is that while I have the opportunity to know where some of my food comes from and to engage in its production, it seems right to do that. And while some of my food is coming from animal death, it seems right to me not to so distance myself from that death that I can forget it and think of my meat as coming to me pain-free. I cannot easily justify the suffering of fish when I catch them, but then, I cannot easily justify the suffering of whatever animal wound up as that grizzled piece of mystery meat on my pizza, nor of the deer that died to boost the production of apples in my favorite orchard. The difference is that I have intimate familiarity with one of them, and I have held its life in my hands.[18]

There is a much bigger picture to be drawn, as well. In holding its life, and many other lives like it, in my hands, I have come to know not just this one fish but the place where the fish live.[19] The fish are connected to one another and to their whole ecosystem. It is worth reminding ourselves that the prefix "eco-" in *ecosystem* and *ecology* comes from Greek *oikos*, meaning "dwelling-place" or "home." The home that the fish represent is my home, too.

The hunter and the fisher, like other people who regularly observe nature, are people who are in a position to notice when things change. If you go to someone's home, you may or may not notice if some furniture has been moved. If it was a big piece, there may be dimples in the carpet where the feet of the furniture had rested—or there may not be. Other changes will not be as evident unless they are dramatic. But in your own home you are likely to notice subtle changes that others miss entirely. It is only with the familiarity that comes with frequent observation that we develop that kind of seeing. This is one of the reasons we have lab components in language and science classes, why we study abroad, why nurses, doctors, and teachers have practicums, why business students have internships: the abstract takes on new life when we observe it empirically and try to engage it in its materiality. This is the old idea of apprenticeship, the kind of learning that comes when you immerse yourself in what you want to know, giving your bones and sinews over to the learning. Some things we only learn through the intense attention of repeated and sustained vital contact. I once asked my environmental philosophy class, "How many kinds of ducks live in our state?" The best (and funniest) answer I got was this: "Two: mallards and non-mallards." By contrast, my duck-hunting buddies Dan and Ben can identify a dozen species of ducks by their calls in the dark or by the pattern of their flight when they still look to me like a faint line on the horizon. They know males from females in flight, and they know what each kind eats, and where it lives.

In most European languages, there are two different verbs that mean "to know." One of them usually means the knowledge of facts, while the other means the knowledge of familiarity. When we move from the abstract kind of knowing (what the Germans call *Wissenschaft*) to the concrete and experiential kind of knowing (what the Germans call *Kenntnis*), we are not merely engaging in an exercise that repeats in the lab what we already learned in the lecture. Rather, we are seeing things in the world in an entirely new way that translates inert abstractions into living realities. Those of us who spend our lives educating others know that you cannot substitute one of these kinds of knowledge for another.

Still, Matthew's question troubled me as I paddled along, and my answer to him seemed somehow inadequate, even as it does today. I think there is more to it than that, that it cannot be about mere census-taking. Surely Ontario's provincial biologists can do all the census-taking that is necessary to allow the government to take appropriate steps to manage the environment of Lake Muskoka? Who am I kidding if I think that my personal census-taking of one narrow channel in a lake that is ten miles long has any relevance at all?

I was approaching our boathouse, so I reeled in my line, tucked the rod into the straps on my bow, and paddled ashore. Matthew met me and walked with me to the boathouse as I went to put away my paddle and lifejacket. Once they were hung up, we strolled to the end of the dock and Matthew pulled up his minnow trap. This is a simple wire trap of the kind that people have been using for millennia: it is a short wire tube with an inverted cone at each end. The fish can swim into the cones, which funnel them in, but they have a hard time finding the way back out once they're in. Matthew usually catches a few small panfish: juvenile rock bass, bluegills and crappies, mostly, though once in a while he'll also find a crayfish.

"What's that?" he asked me. I looked down at the trap and there inside it was a brown fish that looked like a cross between an eel and a catfish, maybe six or seven inches long. It had an ancient and snakelike look to it, and it was something neither of us had expected to see there. Matthew was fascinated, and so was I. I knew right away what it was. "It's a cusk," I told him. "I had no idea there were any cusk in this lake." I have only seen one other cusk in my life, one I caught through the ice in Maine ten years ago, accidentally, while fishing for trout. But that first cusk, in its antediluvian alienness, left a deep impression on my soul. We stared at the fish in wonder for a few moments before releasing it. "Neither did I," he said, his voice hushed with the kind of reverence we save for moments of wonder. Now we knew the answer to his question.

Chapter 5

North Carolina and Tennessee
Moving Mountains

David O'Hara

Whether we live by the seaside, or by the lakes and rivers, or on the prairie, it concerns us to attend to the nature of fishes, since they are not phenomena confined to certain localities only, but forms and phases of the life in nature universally dispersed.

—HENRY DAVID THOREAU,
A WEEK ON THE CONCORD AND MERRIMACK RIVERS

SO MUCH HAPPENS AT the periphery of our vision, so much goes unnoticed as we drive by. We catch glimpses in the corner of our eye, but the faster we're moving, the less time we have to give the things glimpsed. The more life accelerates, the more we filter out. Scenes flash by, and in the city signs and ads become flashier and brighter to try to attract our jaded attention. Sometimes I feel like I don't have time to see anything at all. Once, while driving across the country, I said to my wife that the best thing that ever happened to Nebraska was the interstate, because it allows you to get out of Nebraska faster. I was tired of driving and I was feeling a bit resentful of just how much farther we had to drive. I felt as though the prairie were a thing to be overcome, not a place to be cherished. The irony is that the faster I drive across it, the more uniform it appears, the less of its beauty I allow myself to see. And the less I see of its beauty, the plainer it looks. I now know that Nebraska is a lovely place, but I veil its loveliness with my gauzy inattention, making it a boring background blur that flies by at seventy miles an hour.

Last year, while hunting pheasants in late October, I made an experiment. My hunting buddy, Dan Engebretson, was looking for his young dog, Finn. Finn had given up on pheasants and had decided to run off after a jackrabbit. Given the jackrabbit's energy and the dog's single-mindedness, I knew that retrieving Finn was not going to be a simple operation. While I was waiting for Dan to return, I lay down on my belly and parted the tall grass with my fingers to look for invertebrates that might still be active in cold weather. I thought I might find one or two at most. As I looked at the thirty or forty square inches in front of me, I found over a dozen species still moving around, including spiders, a centipede, and a number of insects, most of them so tiny I couldn't see them until they moved a little in the sunlight. The prairie always amazes me when I allow myself to slow down and see it closely. Your first trip to the prairie might make you think it's empty, and if you drive through at highway speeds, you can leave the prairie with that initial impression unchanged. But the fact is that there's a remarkable abundance of life in the grasslands. If I allow myself to slow down and look, under the appearance of drab uniformity I come to see a rich palette of colors, plants, animals, and soils.

Later Matthew and I trek to the Smoky Mountains. Our trip is an attempt to do something similar to what I did when I lay down in the grass while waiting for Dan to find Finn: we wanted to slow ourselves down and look closely at the watersheds there, to make ourselves available to see what there is to see.

THE SNAKES OF NORTH CAROLINA

As we drive along a smooth dirt road in the Nantahala National Forest, we come upon a long, black snake lying on the road in front of the car. It's a large rat snake, and it must be at least four feet long. We stop and get out of the car to look at it. We're here for the fish, but I'm easily distracted, and I'm driving. Sometimes when we're on fishing trips I forget to fish because I'm so interested in the insects in the air, the trees, the mist, the local secondhand bookstore—you name it. I've occasionally had guides yell at me to wake me from my reveries as fish after fish takes the nymph I am drifting and then spits it out. The fishing brings me to the river or the forest, but then the forest and the river claim my attention.

The rat snake eyes us languidly and glides on a bit. We walk after it and it turns to face us. It is plainly suggesting that while it's not exactly in a rush to have us move on, its tolerance of our proximity has real limits. We're fascinated, but we also want to keep our distance, because we really don't know much about rat snakes. Better safe than sorry. We reluctantly get back in the car and drive on around the snake, leaving it to its sunbathing. We're not really sure we're on the right road. Looking at the snake was partly a distraction from our awareness of this fact, but now we are faced with it again. Matthew consults his directions and his copy of *The North Carolina Atlas and Gazeteer*. Yeah, we're lost.

We've been looking for a small river, a stream, really, one where we've been told there are native brook trout. For the last few nights we've been camping with Matt's brother Ted and Ted's sons, Brad and Michael. From our rustic campsite just below the Fontana Dam on the Cheoah Reservoir we've been exploring the trout waters of the North Carolina mountains. We are in the heart of the Smoky Mountains, which I think is one of the most beautiful places on earth, and one of the most challenging places to drive. Everything here is serpentine, and it moves at its own pace. Roads twist and turn as they follow the path of least resistance, just like the rivers. The roads here don't seem to be made to make driving easy so much as in strict obedience to the lines laid down by the mountains, and those lines are rarely straight for long. There's a road that runs from Tellico Lake to the Cheoah Dam. It winds so much—dozens of times each mile—that the motorcyclists who come here to ride its tight undulations call it the "Tail of the Dragon," adding to the serpentine imagery of these valleys.

The Smokies rise out of the plains of eastern Tennessee and form much of western North Carolina. They boast some of the highest peaks in the Appalachians. They create their own weather, forcing the warm, wet air that blows from the west upward into cooler air that condenses it into the smoky clouds that gave the mountains their name. Clouds drift through the mountains, alternately concealing and disclosing high peaks and steep valleys, giving constant variation to the vistas, feather boas of mist wending tranquil paths through the mountains, going where they will. This is a wonderful place.

So far the fishing has been fine, but all we've seen have been big, fat rainbow trout we caught while wading in the Cheoah River upstream of its confluence with the Little Tennessee River. The rainbows have been fun to catch because they take a fly aggressively in these fast waters, and they're good fighters. I'm not sure why fishers like fish that fight hard, but we do. Big brown trout will sometimes plunge to the bottom of a pool with remarkable power and "sit" there, resisting all attempts to haul them up; by contrast, rainbows will often launch themselves out of the water in wild arcs, flipping their heads as they do when climbing waterfalls, or "tailwalking" on the surface of the water. More than a few times I've hooked a rainbow trout only to have it shake the fly free a moment later when it leapt from the water.

Ted's son Michael is preparing for a few weeks of living off the land in the nearby Slick Rock Wilderness Area in the Nantahala National Forest. He's bringing nothing with him except a knife, a fishing rod, a sleeping bag, and a little .22 caliber rifle for small game. He's confident that the land here has plenty of food and water to offer him, and as he lectures to me about the culinary virtues of kudzu and nettles, I begin to believe he'll be just fine. (As we found out later, he never needed to use the gun to hunt small game; the plants and the local trout provided him with ample food each day.) We join him in some of his preparations by keeping a few of these rainbows and cooking them over an open fire. We cook them whole, on sticks, and eat them plain—nothing but trout. The fish fall apart in neat filets once they're cooked, leaving a skeleton that looks like one of those cartoon fish skeletons a cat has licked clean. The meat is light and flaky, with just a little fat. An hour earlier this fish was swimming, and now it's melting in my mouth. I'm not sure fish has ever tasted so good. But like I said, even though these fish have delighted us, we'd really like to see the native trout, the brookies, and that's why we're lost today.

Our situation is funny, actually, because Matthew and I both love maps, so you'd think we'd be able to follow one to our destination. As kids we spent hours gazing at world maps, road maps, any maps we could get access to. In college I worked for a federal repository library, often in the map room, sorting and filing USGS maps. I admit I did that part of my job slowly, because I loved to look at the maps and to trace the watersheds, to follow the contour lines and imagine from these two-dimensional lines the soaring cliffs or steep plunging valleys where blue water coursed and fish leapt. It turns out that loving maps does not prevent one from misreading them, especially in such twisting terrain. Theory and practice don't always go hand in hand, I guess. After another half hour of retracing our steps and turning maps around and around, we find what we're looking for: the upper reaches of the Santeetlah River.

Matthew and I grew up in places where brook trout thrive. The further north you go, the bigger the fish and the bigger the populations. Here, as we approach the southern end of the Appalachians, trout become smaller and scarcer. We've found brook trout as far south as the mountains in the northwest corner of South Carolina and the northeast corner of Georgia, but in those places they are few and far between. In the early 1900s rainbow trout like the ones we were catching on the Cheoah were introduced throughout much of the range of the native southern brook trout. Generally speaking, trout aren't unwanted invasive species like zebra mussels, Eurasian milfoil, or Asian carp. Native trout will migrate upstream or downstream a bit, but they tend to stay where they are placed by nature. Those trout that live in large lakes or the sea tend to return to their native streams to reproduce, and those that live only in small streams or rivers have no opportunity to move to other waters. In pretty much every instance, trout are invasive because we have transplanted them. Our species loves trout, so when we find water we think they'd like, we often put them there. They're attractive party-crashers, and most people are reluctant to kick them out when they show up uninvited. Thanks to all this transplanting, I'm told it is now possible to catch trout in all fifty U.S. states, even though only about half of the states have indigenous salmonid populations. There are even wild trout in Hawaii. Rainbow trout were introduced there in 1920 and restocked repeatedly throughout much of the twentieth century. Like so many others who visit Hawaii, they've found a comfortable niche and have taken up permanent residence. Several other salmonids, including brook trout and Chinook salmon, have also been introduced to Hawaii at various times. The persistence of trout in Hawaii illustrates the fact that nonnative fish can adapt to a fairly wide range of conditions. Sudden changes, like a rapid and dramatic change in water quality or the introduction of a new species, are hard for native fish to adapt to. Too frequently, the transplants outcompete the natives and the native populations collapse.

You'd think that the brookies, being the indigenous species in the Appalachians, would be better adapted to the region and that they would outcompete the rainbows, but rainbows have actually displaced the brookies throughout much of their southern range. Kurt Fausch, a biologist at

Colorado State University, has been studying brook trout for several decades. He has told me that this displacement of the brookies by rainbows is probably due to several factors, one of which is that in the South, brook trout live at the limits of what they are adapted to, meaning that it doesn't take much to tip the scales against them. They need cold, clear water, and they aren't as well adapted to warm, rainy winters as the rainbows transplanted here from their native western range. (Ironically, brook trout that have been transplanted in the western states have had the same effect on indigenous cutthroat trout as rainbows have had on brookies in the southern Appalachians.) To find indigenous brook trout in this region you often have to go far upstream, above natural barriers that rainbows can't cross, to tiny streams like the far reaches of the upper Santeetlah.

We stop the car by the side of the road and walk onto the one-lane bridge. We sit down on the bridge and look down at the shallow, clear water running out from under our feet. It looks like it could support trout, though they're sure to be both small and sparsely distributed.

Matthew and I get out our seven-foot-long three-weight fly rods, small rods for small streams with tight casting conditions and small fish. Mine is a two-piece Diamondback handmade for me by my friend Mike Burris, who used to work in the Diamondback workshop in Vermont. It's light and forgiving and great for snapping flies into very tight spots. It was a beautiful gift, one that makes me think of Mike whenever I use it. For me, fly fishing is a practice of remembering connections. When I cast I remember the first bamboo rod my father gave me, and how he taught me to cast it on the upper reaches of the Hudson river in the heart of the Adirondack Mountains of New York. Tying knots frequently reminds me of the men who taught me to make strong, efficient connections between hooks and lines. Many of my flies were tied by now distant friends, but using their handiwork makes them feel near. Fly-fishing is a solitary practice, but it depends on a whole community for its possibility. Few of us can ever claim to fish completely alone. We fish constantly in the presence of those who have taught us, a great cloud of witnesses watching our every cast.

Matthew and I tie on small, light mayfly imitations that sit high on the water and look like subimago flies getting ready to take wing, molt again, and mate. The mayflies are a favorite food of trout. We step into the stream and the cool water feels good on our feet. Matthew walks ahead a little and I stay back and watch as he carefully casts under low-hanging branches. After he takes a few casts, I pass him and walk to the next pool. We continue up the stream, leapfrogging one another and trying to keep a low profile, because trout in shallow water are easily spooked. If they see us, they'll dart for cover and won't come out for a long time. We get only one or two casts per pool, so we try to make them count. It takes us about half an hour to find our first trout. Streams like this, even when they are very healthy, do not support many fish, and those that live in these streams tend not to grow very big. An eight-inch trout can be a lunker in mountain headwaters like the one we're fishing. They grow slowly in these waters, and if they grow too large they become easy prey for birds and mammals when the water gets low.

The trout populations in these streams are fragile and easily disrupted. Several times in our years of fishing together Matthew and I have had similar conversations with local fishers. We ask, "How's the fishing?" And they reply, "Well, last year it was great. My kids and I pulled out fifty trout in a single day on this river. But we haven't seen a trout in here since then." What they never seem to realize is that in that one day of bounty, they probably caught every fish in that section of the stream. If that section is bounded by waterfalls, they may have just eliminated the brook trout population altogether. They've squandered their inheritance in prodigal angling, and now their streams are empty. In any event, they have certainly done harm that can take years to repair. When I hear it, I am heartbroken. But it is understandable why people take out so many fish. It is fun to catch them, after all, and they are good food.

What makes an even bigger difference for trout is legislation that attempts to balance the competing aims of managing fish populations, generating revenue for both states and private businesses, and pleasing voters who like to fish. The assumption of many state regulatory bodies seems to be that if people are told they cannot keep any fish, fewer people will fish in your state. And, of course, if you tell people they can't take home many fish, you might lose their vote on the next election day. On the other hand—the assumption continues—if creel limits are generous, anglers will take that as a sign of a thriving fishery and will come visit your state, spending money on guides and hotels, thus adding to tax revenue. Local anglers will also spend more money on licenses, at tackle shops, and at local restaurants. Set aside for a moment the question of whether this assumption is sound. It is at any rate one of the main reasons for state-run fish hatcheries, which serve to support "put-and-take" angling. The state puts the fish in the rivers, and anglers take them out. In lakes, ponds, and lower reaches of bigger rivers, this is often a workable strategy—especially if previous management efforts have already destroyed the indigenous fish population. In those places, there is enough water to support the hundreds of fish that may be dumped into the water from a hatchery truck. On little streams, there simply isn't enough water to support many more fish, and anything more than a very modest harvest of fish from these waters could do serious harm to their population. This makes the production of browns and rainbows—which are fairly easy to breed and which thrive in bigger waters—easier and more attractive than the production of smaller native brook trout. Managing trout, and trout water, is not a simple matter.

Fortunately, fishing itself tends to make things simpler, to uncomplicate life for a little while. We're not the first ones to remark that many of us who fish are only ostensibly seeking fish. The fish are the outward thing, the visible sign, the necessary tangibles that mediate some other relationship. We're also not the first ones to note that when a group of people love some species of plant or animal, they work to preserve it, often with the side benefit of conserving whole ecosystems along with it.

Ahead of us a thick fallen tree lies on its side, its roots jutting out into the stream. The roots narrow the stream, concentrating its force. As the current passes the roots it swirls around behind them and there it has carved out a deep hole, perhaps two feet deep in a stream that is otherwise barely deep enough to reach the tops of our boots. Matthew flicks his fly perfectly under the tree and into the riffle just upstream of the hole, where the current tumbles down over small round stones into the deep water. The fly drifts off the riffle into the deep slack water of the undercut bank. Brook trout in small streams are opportunistic feeders, and for good reason. They tend to lie in slow, deep water where they have a good view of fast-moving water in the nearby current. The slow water allows them to rest while watching for food in the fast-moving water buffet beside them. If something that looks like food floats by, they have only a moment to decide whether it's food or not. While fishing under stands of hemlock trees we have occasionally caught brook trout with their mouths full of hemlock needles. Either the fish were trying to poison themselves in imitation of Socrates or they mistook the needles for small terrestrial insects that had fallen into the stream, and, making a quick decision, chose to eat the needles. The latter seems the likelier story.

As soon as Matt's fly exits the current, a small but plump brook trout slips out of its hiding spot and sips Matt's fly off the surface. Matthew lifts the rod tip slightly and hooks the fish. He plays it quickly and brings it downstream to his feet. Holding his rod high in his left hand, he moistens his right hand in the stream and then uses it to cradle the fish gently while he slackens the line. The brookie's colors are the colors of the Smoky Mountains: its back and sides are vermiculated with winding patterns of varying shades of deep green, dappled like sunlight dapples the forest floor. Looking at a live brook trout is like reading a Gerard Manley Hopkins poem; vibrant life springs out everywhere. Just as these trees will change throughout the seasons, so the greens on this fish give way to soft gold and fiery red, its ventral fins streaked with creamy white. We look at it for only a moment, and then the barbless hook slips smoothly from its jaw. Matthew continues to cradle it without putting any pressure on it, and its body undulates in the river as it swims over his hand for a moment, catching its liquid breath before it darts back to its hiding spot.

Satisfied with having found a brook trout, I now give my attention to the other life in the stream, turning over rocks and looking along the banks. A good deal of sunlight filters through the forest canopy, and the banks are lined with grasses and short plants I don't recognize. Most fly fishers know that it's not a bad idea to have a few flies tied to imitate ants, because just about everywhere there are trout, there are ants, and they are in plentiful supply here, too. There are also plentiful orb-weaving spiders, jumping spiders, and wolf spiders. Under the rocks I find a few caddisflies and a few mayflies, but they are not abundant. The insects that live in a stream are one of the threads that tie trout to many other nearby species, including spiders, reptiles, bats, and birds. Each of these may prey on aquatic insects, which means that a change in stream ecology may very quickly have broad local effects on other species. I take a water sample and test the pH. It's low, but within tolerable limits. These mountain streams are often slightly acidic because the leaf debris on the forest floor has an acidifying effect as tannins leach from decaying leaves into groundwater. Also, this high up in the mountains, rainwater simply hasn't been underground very long when it enters the stream, so if it is acidic when it falls from the sky (as it often is downwind of industrial cities) it has not had much time to be buffered by minerals on the ground.

Crane flies and mosquitoes drift lazily in the midday warmth. As we walk back to the car, dozens of small pale-blue butterflies gather in tight clusters to sip at exposed minerals on the ground. Several much larger but-terflies, black and dark blue with lines of white and orange spots, join them in this mineral feast. This is one of those delights of walking in the woods. Unpaved roads can sometimes provide essential nutrients and habitat for woodland creatures. Often in the evening you can find birds on the road gathering stones for their crops to help them crush and digest their evening meal. Lacking teeth with which to grind what they eat, they mill their food further down their digestive tract, and gravel roads provide a perfect source for the gravel they need. The butterflies are seeking salt and other mineral nutrients. And the rat snake we saw earlier in the day was probably sunning itself to warm itself up for its morning hunt.

TELLICO RIVER WATERSHED, TENNESSEE

We stay as long as we dare, but we want to get moving while we have sun-light. The next leg of our trip takes us to eastern Tennessee, which means we have the pleasure of driving the Cherohala Scenic Skyway, a beautiful two-lane road that connects the Nantahala National Forest and the Cher-okee National Forest. "Scenic Skyway" is a good name for this road; for a little while it lifts you out of the valleys of the Smokies and brings you to the top of the mountains, following their ridges. Building roads in the mountains is tricky business, and the results are often ugly scars across the mountain face. Here I feel like I'm being treated to the work of engineers who thought first of beauty and of submission to the contours of the land, then only later about speed. This is not a road to hasten you on your way; it is a road that is both a means of transit and a beautiful end in itself. We glide over the mountains at a leisurely pace, and begin to coast down into eastern Tennessee.

We're headed for the town of Tellico Plains, where we'll meet a guide who will take us on the upper Tellico River. The Tellico River is a little more than fifty miles long, many of those miles suitable for trout. This is the longest free-flowing coldwater river in Tennessee. It's also one of the most heavily fished and heavily managed put-and-take trout streams we've visited. One state biologist we spoke to described the lower Tellico as "a circus." Every week from mid-March to mid-September, stocking trucks full of hatchery-raised rainbow trout drive along the river, stopping to pour in trout for an-glers to catch. Something like 135,000 trout are put into it every year, most of which are promptly taken out by anglers. The river is closed to fishing two days a week for stocking, presumably both to give the stocking trucks time to work and to prevent anglers from following the trucks and removing the fish right after they're placed in the water. Each week on the day it reopens the lower Tellico becomes a fish market. People line the banks to fill their creels with fish that have lived in the river for only a day or two.

Upstream of this circus, in its headwaters, the Tellico gathers the rain that falls on a broad swath of mountains, carrying that water down from the Smokies toward the Tennessee River. The Tennessee, together with the Cumberland, drains most of Tennessee. Water from the Tellico eventually flows through Tennessee and south into Alabama, watering cities like Chattanooga and Huntsville, before turning north again, to cross Tennessee a second time, flowing parallel to the Cumberland for a short while before both rivers join the Ohio River. The Tellico gained notoriety in the 1970s when it gave its name to the infamous Tellico Dam, the dam that impounded the waters of the Tellico and the Little Tennessee rivers in the Tellico Reservoir, flooding native American historical sites and endangering the snail darter, a small river fish that most people had never heard of until it became a political byword.

In the springtime, the Tellico boasts some class IV whitewater, some of the best—and roughest—water available for kayakers. Its major tributaries include the Bald River, with its majestic falls, and the North River. The Tellico is a powerful river, and when it floods, it floods hard. The banks give us a view of how high the floodwaters can get. Building bridges here takes careful engineering. The steep sides of the Smokies concentrate rainfall and snowmelt into narrow channels, and calm rivers can quickly become torrents.

In the 1880s clear-cutting timber harvest began in earnest in this region. By the early 1900s a railroad reached Tellico Plains to allow the fine Tennessee hardwoods that covered these mountains to be carted away to build homes in Michigan. The timber baron who brought the logging operation here promised that he wouldn't leave a stick standing in his efforts to turn the forest into capital, and he very nearly kept his promise. One logger said of these hills, "all we want to do is get the most we can out of this country, as quickly as we can, and get out."[20]

When you remove the trees, floods happen more quickly. Rain that would have coated leaves and soaked bark, rain that would have been absorbed by the debris on the forest floor, and rain that would have been drawn up into root and branch, simply runs downhill with nothing to impede it. The soil and leaf debris are carried away into the river, which is bad news for anything that breathes clear water, like hellbenders and trout, or for anything that needs unsilted beds for its eggs and young—again, like trout, and like the riverine benthic invertebrates. Fine sediment suspended in the water fouls the gills of trout and suffocates them, like smoky air does to creatures with lungs. Trout can ride out brief periods of muddy water if they can find less silty slack water to hide in, but a lot of runoff will kill trout quickly. Not much survived in the Tellico once the logging began. When it rained—and it rains a lot in the Smokies—the rivers turned from clear glass to chocolate milk, and the bodies of trout floated downstream, their gills full of suffocating mud and their white bellies turned to face the sun. "Splash dams" made the flooding worse. To get the logs downstream more efficiently, loggers on the Tellico built temporary dams that could form deep holding ponds for logs. As the dams filled, the stream below became a trickle, exposing natural cover. When the ponds were full, the dams were opened abruptly, sending a devastating wave of lumber and water that scoured the river and swept away everything in its path. This logging and flooding happened not just in the Tellico but throughout a great swath of the Smoky Mountains. Between roughly 1900 and 1935, many of the native brook trout populations of the southern Appalachians were completely destroyed by logging operations.

We humans may cause a lot of harm, but we also often recognize it when we have, and sometimes we try to make it right. Eventually, upstream calamities become evident downstream. And the people of Tellico Plains were not indifferent to the abuse of their watershed. In 1901 a newspaper editorial in Tellico Plains protested that "the general government ought to step in before it is too late. If the timber is all stripped from these hills the streams will dry up and the ultimate loss will be serious and widespread." That voice crying out in the wilderness was eventually heard. In 1911 the Weeks Act authorized purchase of forested or once-forested land in the watersheds of navigable rivers to preserve and restore these important waters. Thus began the acquisition of what was to become the Cherokee National Forest in 1920. Of course, sometimes our medicines can be worse than the disease, or they can have unwanted side effects. Around the same time as the Weeks Act state fisheries officials found it easier to replace the lost native brook trout with rainbow trout imported from western states, since rainbows are much easier to breed and stock. Even where the brook trout survived the logging, the rainbows outcompeted them, and the numbers of brook trout continued to decline as the rainbows migrated upstream throughout the watershed.[21] The attempt to restore the fishery partly helped the beleaguered native brook trout by restoring its habitat. But when we rebuilt its house, we put a few gorillas in its living room, and then told it to sit down and make itself at home. It's probably possible to share a house with apes, but don't expect them to share your food with you. You'll probably move out quickly, which is what the brook trout have done.

So we've come to the Tellico for two reasons. First, we're still looking for native southern brook trout. The most remote headwaters of the Tellico are said to still hold a small but significant population of the southern strain of indigenous brook trout. Second, we're looking for hope, and the lower Tellico offers us a picture of what a trout river can look like after it has been restored, even if it has become a rainbow trout river. The once ravaged mountains have been reforested and the river is now managed as an active fishery. We'd like to see what that looks like, and what we can learn from it.

After putting our bags in the cabin we've rented, Matthew and I head out to look at the river. We have a little time, so we drive back upstream to the village of Green Cove. We've been told that the woman who runs the convenience store at the Green Cove Motel has a wealth of local fishing lore, and we're eager to meet her. The building looks like it has been here a long time; it has that settled look, like the way boulders, deposited in the forest by glaciers or having rolled down a mountainside centuries ago, look both natural and a little bit alien. And like boulders, the cabins of the motel look like they've been worn and weathered by years of forest rain. Green Cove is a quiet, shady, restful place.

Just behind the store, the river slopes and chatters down the rocks. The store caters to forgetful anglers by supplying them with basic groceries and basic fishing gear. Marshmallows, chocolate, and graham crackers for campfire s'mores. Peanut butter and bread, and Twinkies. Nets that look far too big for use on a mountain stream. On the shelf beside the counter is a set of clear plastic drawers full of hand-tied flies. Yellow and black seem to be predominant colors in the dry flies.

We spend the next half hour talking with Catherine, the woman who has run the store since 1964. When we ask about trout, she smiles and her eyes shine. Without the trout, there might be no Green Cove. People come here to fish, and faded photos of happy anglers and their trout adorn the walls. She tells us the fishing is so good because the river is stocked every week. In fact, the stocking truck puts fish in right here, right behind the store. Matthew and I steal glances out the back window. It's true—even from here, you can see them in the pools. One long trout rises gently to take something from the surface of the river. Only guests of the motel are allowed to access the river here. Since we aren't guests of the motel, we ask where else people fish around here. She looks a bit confused by the question, then admits she doesn't know. But the fishing here is good, so why go somewhere else? In a way, the stocking truck that brings the fish brings with it the lifeblood of Green Cove.

The story takes a slightly melancholy turn when she tells us that the store is for sale. She tells us she's in her eighties now. She just doesn't have the energy to keep up with it, she says, though she seems full of life here beside this river. Folks around here and her regular visitors don't want her to sell the store, because they don't want the change. The Green Cove Motel is a tradition, an institution. It is a part of the Tellico, the place where many people from near and far away step into the river and experience its life. Her eyes, focused on something distant, gaze downstream.

Early the next morning we meet our guide, Mark Scarborough, at a gas station and convenience store at the end of the Cherohala Scenic Skyway in Tellico Plain. We met Mark through Dane Law at Southeastern Anglers, a guide service we found online. Mark tells us that he and Dane had a hard time believing that two Northerners wanted to hire him to guide them into brook trout water. The lower Tellico's full of plump, stocked rainbow trout, and it's famous for producing big brown trout as well. There are tales around here of twenty-pound brown trout being pulled out of the lower Tellico. Everyone we talk to seems to know the same stories. Big browns lurk in the swift, rocky holes downstream. Just as in North Carolina, the rainbows thrive here. So why would anyone want to fish and write about the native brookies? Mark says, "When we got your email we thought about having Snuffy Smith meet you at the store this morning." He laughs at the idea of two Yankees trying to communicate with a gruff eastern Tennessee woodsman. I laugh out loud with him, and shiver a little.

Mark drives us upriver to the upper Bald River, one of the tributaries of the Tellico. The Bald River is one of the few places where the unique southern strain of brook trout were found by the fisheries biologists who have worked to restore them.

Mark is affable, and full of information and stories. A ruffed grouse runs across the road in front of the truck. "Mountain chicken!" Mark says. "Good eating." As we drive he points to trees we pass. The road is steep, and the trees stand tall and straight. Hemlock, chestnut, and white pine grow here, just as they did in the days before the clear-cutting. Now yellow poplar, white and red oak, hemlock and some sycamore make up a good portion of the canopy. It looks like native forest, but Mark's woodsman eyes see both what is old and what is new here. "Sassafrass," he says, pointing to one tree with tri-lobed leaves. "The wood is strong, light, and flexible. Good canoe paddles are made from it." The forest is not just landscape; it is a place of rich resources, full of life and utility and possibility. Mark tells us that the Cherokees would catch brook trout by dumping hemlock branches into a pool. The mild toxins in the branches would stun the fish, which would float to the surface where they could be picked up. Not very sporting, perhaps, but far less toxic than many of the things we do to rivers today. I'm not sure whether Mark's story falls under the heading of "stories" or "information," but it doesn't really matter to me right now.

The hood ornament on Mark's truck is an angler made from colorful twisted wire. Mark says he used to live in the back of his pickup truck, but marriage put an end to that. Now his truck is full of fishing gear and flies. I often worry about leaving my car unattended in remote spots. I lost my wallet once when I left it in a car in rural Massachusetts while fishing with a friend. In a place where it seemed there were no other people, someone found our car, broke in, and took my wallet. Once bitten, twice shy—now I'm wary of where I park, and I don't leave anything in plain sight in the car. Mark, on the other hand, doesn't seem concerned about someone breaking into the truck while he's guiding us. I suspect that's because everyone knows him here. Or perhaps he just trusts the people around here to do the right thing. He tells me he and his wife have made the decision to live as though money didn't matter. There's something spiritual and appealing about his attitude. Here in the woods, he seems solid, rooted, at home like the chestnut trees. He's not naïve, or ignorant. As he talks about the forest, he rattles off the Latin taxonomic names of plants as easily as I can name my friends. His simple demeanor conceals profound local knowledge. It's not the first time that I, a college professor, feel like a young student again; our guide is the professor, and the forest and streams are his classroom.

As we drive up into the mountains, we backtrack along the Cherohala Skyway at first, but then we head off on smaller roads, and finally we're bouncing along wet dirt roads and moving fast. Mark plainly knows these roads well, and he's eager to get us to the water. Along the way, he rattles off information about local fish, the kinds of trees we're passing, birds, and other fauna. I recall a guidebook I read about this area that described it as "bear-infested," and I ask Mark about that. He does nothing to allay my fears. "Yeah, there's a lot of bears in here." We ride, bumping in his truck as he speaks. "But they're not nearly as dangerous as the Russian boars," he offers cheerfully. "They'll tear you apart." He smiles. Like I said, he is affable.

We come down a hill and cross a little bridge, and Mark parks the truck. The air is warm and wet. The water is cold, and it feels good on our legs. The stream is twenty feet wide in places, giving us room to cast with our short fly rods, but the water is clear and the fish are wary of anything that moves along the banks. We approach each hole as stealthily as we can. Heavy forest canopy and the gray sky help considerably.

As we walk, Mark alternates between giving us fishing tips and telling us more stories. He was with a group of guides who once guided President Carter on a rafting trip through the Smokies. He asked too many questions of the Secret Service on that trip, so they kicked him off his own raft. I'm curious, so I ask, "What did you ask them?"

"All I asked them was, 'What's in those boxes?'" he says. "I guess it must have been something important, 'cause they sure didn't want me on that raft anymore." He smiles broadly, obviously pleased with the memory. He doesn't seem to have any rancor about being evicted from his own boat; he is at ease in the world.

He does have his secrets, of course, as every good guide does. And like the president's guards, he has his secret weapons. Some of them he can't use anymore. He tells us about the old days when yellowhammer flies could be made from real yellowhammer feathers. The yellowhammer is a kind of flicker which is, like all passerine birds, a protected species. Even though every child likes to pick up feathers from the ground, fishing guides need to exercise care, because technically it is a violation of federal law to harvest and possess the feathers of protected birds. Game wardens have cracked down on people possessing actual yellowhammer feathers recently. The yellowhammer is the key to catching trout in the Tellico watershed, but now that it has to be tied with dyed rooster feathers it's just not the same as the old days, he says wistfully. He hands me one of the new, legal yellowhammers, and I tie it on. I'm surprised the way his story makes me feel like the fly in my hand—which otherwise looks like a fine fly—is a cheap imitation.

We wade upstream a bit, then take to the trail to hike further upstream. Everything is wet here. The trail is slick mud at times. Our wading boots don't help. In the stream, the fibers of the felt soles we used to wear would cling to slick rocks like Velcro, but on muddy trails all they do is gather enough mud to become heavy and as slick as the trail. We slip and slide our way up along the edge of the river. All around us are huge rhododendrons along the banks. Their twisted stems grow like woody vines, thirty feet in the air, stretching out over the river to give impenetrable cover to the fish.

We fish a few holes as we head upstream, but our goal is above a waterfall, ten or twelve feet high. This waterfall is too high for rainbows to jump. The pool below holds several rainbows, and they, in turn, hold our attention for a little while. After we catch and release some of them, we start up a steep section of trail that leads us above the falls. Now we are reaching our goal—native brook trout territory.

Here the river becomes even harder to fish as it begins to fork into smaller streams. Rhododendrons and fallen logs reach across the stream every few yards, making it harder to cast, and making it hard to land fish when we do hook them. We hike up alongside more stairstep falls and we come to a stream that is simply uncastable. The stream is entirely covered with branches from one bank to the other and without any breaks. It flows through a low cavern of bushes and trees, and its deep pools are inaccessible from above. We are now well above the range of the rainbow trout, and Mark points under the branches. "That's where you'll find your native brookies." I look at him, incredulous. The water looks deep enough to hold trout, but it also looks unfishable. As a boy I sometimes fished under heavy branches by floating a baited hook downstream. I'd crawl up to a hole on a trout stream and drop my line in the water, lying on a rock and peering over the edge to watch the bait drift downstream and waiting for the line to straighten with the sudden tension of a brook trout's strike.

But this is different, because there is no point upstream that we can get to, and there's no way to cast upstream. I guess Mark can read my face, because he is smiling. "You know how to cast there?" "I have no idea," I reply. He holds out his hand for my rod, and I hand it to him. I've been fishing all my life; what can he show me that I don't know already? He reels in the line until there's only about seven feet of leader coming from the topmost guide on my rod. He kneels down in the stream and points the tip of the rod at a little hole about fifteen feet upstream, under the brush. Taking the light yellow nymph in his left hand, he pulls it back slightly, then lets go. He is using my rod like a slingshot, and the nymph shoots up the length of the rod, landing in the pool where he pointed it. "Just do that," he says, still smiling.

Guiding is an odd business. The people who do it are often people who want to be out hunting and fishing, so they get paid to take other people hunting and fishing, which plainly frustrates some of them, who now find themselves accompanying wealthy people who are doing the thing that they themselves wish they were doing. Mark isn't like that; he seems to delight in being outdoors regardless of whether he's fishing, and he plainly enjoys teaching us and telling us stories. Matthew and I try out our new casting technique, and Mark waves us on. "Take your time. I'll be here when you come back out." The stream forks here, so we each crawl into one of the wooded caverns and begin slingshotting nymphs for trout. Mark plainly has no intention of following us.

We fish this way for half an hour or so, crawling upstream with almost no headroom, our whole bodies soaking in the stream and slipping on smooth, mossy rocks. And each pool holds another tiny native brook trout. These are not trophies by most standards: the big ones are five or six inches long; most are three or four inches long. But they are survivors, and they are beautiful to see in action. They have survived deforestation and predation and have found a place to hide in a stream enrobed by trees. Perhaps they will outlive us up here. Perhaps someday this river will be theirs again. They are biding their time in the deep holes, watching the current, and sipping in the nutrients that flow past them. In half an hour we've covered a few hundred yards at most. We would have gone further, but Mark mentioned that he came upon a bear den not long ago right near here. Rationally, we know black bears aren't likely to bother us. But we're not entirely rational in the woods.

As we walk back down the trail to the truck, Mark tells us how he became a fly fisher. As a boy, he wanted to learn to fish for trout, so he went to a fly shop in Atlanta and asked Sarge, the owner, how to get started. "How much money ya got, kid?" Sarge asked him. Mark had saved sixty dollars. "Walmart will sell you junk for that much," he told Mark. Then he gathered up a thousand dollars' worth of fishing equipment from around the store: a good rod, a reel spooled up with decent floating line, a net, flies, and other necessaries. "Here," Sarge said, "you can borrow this, and learn to fish. Come back when you have a hundred dollars and we'll talk more." Mark took the tackle and learned to use it, and went back to the store as often as he could to learn more, and Sarge gave him more equipment, and more lessons. He took a risky bet in investing in this boy he did not know, and that bet paid off. Sarge made a fly fisherman out of Mark. More importantly, Sarge made Mark into the kind of man who can tell the difference between the value of money and the value of a healthy mountain river. And Sarge made Mark a teacher. Now I feel like Mark is passing on to us the same kind of generosity that was shown to him. Someone who cares about trout is someone worth teaching, worth telling your stories to. The stories that get passed down from generation to generation are more than fish tales, even if a few of the details change. They instruct, and they offer entertainment, but they also offer lessons about how to live with rivers and the things that are connected to them. And, as it turns out, everything is connected to rivers.

The next day Matthew and I decide to explore some other sections of the Bald River and the upper Tellico. We spend the morning driving from place to place, stopping to take pictures of waterfalls and doing a lot of hiking up trails in search of good fishing holes that aren't frequented by many fishers. Everywhere we go, it's obvious that a lot of people here fish for trout. It makes us wonder how many more trout stories we'd hear if we had more time to spend here.

We decide to spend what remains of the day fishing on the upper Bald River again, to see if we can find brook trout on more of its tiny tributaries. We start to hike up the same trails Mark took us on, but then veer off at a place he had suggested and clamber down a steep, wooded slope. Pretty soon we're in deep forest, and every few steps we have to climb over another fallen tree. We can't see more than a few yards in any direction. It's easy to imagine how someone who didn't know the woods could get lost here. We keep heading downhill, towards the water. Off to our right, there's a sharp crack of a broken branch. We both freeze. All I can hear is my heart pounding in my ears as I strain to hear what it is. It sounded like something big. A deer? A bear? A boar? Both of us make quick decisions about which trees we'll climb if a boar charges us. The forest is silent except for the distant sound of running water and birds singing overhead. We wait in silence for a minute but we don't hear anything else. We decide to move on, but our guard is up. A moment later there's another crack, and we freeze again. Silence. We exchange glances, and neither of us wants to move. We wait a while, and there's nothing. We can't stay here forever, so we move on. We don't hear any more branches cracking, but we imagine we do, and we're a bit tense.

Soon we get to the river, and, as rivers so often do, this one makes us forget everything else. We spend the next hour or so working downstream from brookie territory into the rainbows below the falls. A bit below the falls we head back into the woods and angle up toward the trail. We're close to the parking area, only half a mile or so away. We still have a hundred yards or so to go before we get to the trail when something unusual catches my eye. I'm not sure why, but that pile of branches bothers me. It's not natural, not the way branches fall. We move closer to get a better look at it. As we approach, we see a bit of blue tarp under the branches. I lift it up and see some large plastic drums under the tarp. In an instant, curiosity becomes fear, and we step back, looking around us. We haven't seen what's in the barrels, but someone has gone to some trouble to conceal them, which means someone doesn't want us to find them. And we have no idea who— or where—that someone is. We walk quickly and circumspectly toward the trail and back to the rental car. No one has disturbed it, no other car is there. We've been silent as we walked, and the whole place seems shrouded in wonder and mystery. What was the story behind the tarp and the barrels? And do we want to know? Some secrets people are willing to die—or kill—for. Our concern about bears and boars was nothing compared to our concern about what our fellow humans might do if we disturbed their plans.

We came here to see the trout and to see the restored river, but we find that this town has a third reason to make it a good stop for us. We've spent a good deal of time studying the history of brook trout, trying to discover as much as we can about their native range and early spread to these different watersheds. Here, in Tellico Plain, we have found a town that cares a good deal about its history. Hopefully we can find early writings about brook trout. Mark has already given us a lot of oral history, but it would be ideal to find some manuscripts from before the timber cutting began. We visit the Forest Service visitor center, and they have some good historical information about clear-cutting and river restoration. Photos on the wall show the devastation from the logging a century ago, but not much about what preceded that time.

On a hunch, we head over to where some hatchery workers are loading rainbow trout into a hatchery truck. Perhaps they'll be able to tell us more. They eye us with the jaundiced eye of men who are accustomed to being followed by anglers hoping to find out where the fish are stocked.

As they maneuver the heavy six-inch hoses that pump fish into the trucks from the raceways, we explain our project and begin to ask them a few questions. We manage to elicit a few monosyllables, but they're plainly not interested in us. One of them disconnects a hose and three rainbow trout drop out onto the ground. He ignores them, just as he has been ignoring us. Matthew and I quickly scoop up the trout flopping on the hard stones and place them back in the raceways. The truck driver walks past us with the hose and straps it onto the truck, preparing to go to some undisclosed location where he will pump the fish back through the hoses into the river so that anglers can add them to their freezers. I wonder, as he drives off, how many of those trout will get sloshed onto the ground just short of the river. I imagine him kicking them in, or simply walking away and letting them flop there. I suppose that if you work here it is tempting to think of fish as a thing to be pumped through hoses, a commodity to be poured into rivers for ungrateful anglers.

Hoping for a better source of information, or at least a less reticent one, we go back down the road toward Tellico Plain. In town we passed a historical museum, the Charles Hall Museum, and we figure there might be no better place to learn about local history. The museum is one man's *wunderkammer*, a fascinating warehouse of curiosities. The former mayor, who served his town for three decades, a man of no small local influence, has gathered together in a single room his collection of, well, everything. Books and guns, old telephones and cars, photographs, war memorabilia, glass insulators, and all sorts of antiques. It's a small-town marvel. The place fascinates me, and my inner twelve-year-old wants to gaze at the old military equipment for hours. Like a keen-eyed raven, the mayor has collected all things that shine, and the collection is an impressive educational resource for the area. Sadly, we don't find much about trout, but Hall has preserved a sense of the sudden changes that swept through this town when it was forested. Like the Forest Service visitor center, and like the photos on the walls of the Green Cove Motel, it speaks a strong word about the importance of remembering the past.

Before we leave town, I have one last hope: I have to see if there are any secondhand bookstores. Sometimes, like I said, I like to seek distractions that will slow me down. New bookstores are fine if you know what you're looking for, but secondhand bookstores are a good place to look for books you don't yet know. In Tellico Plains there's a little place called The Bookshelf. There might be something there that tells us about the trout here. Matthew and I drive over and browse the shelves. I find a small brown hardcover with a promising title: *In the Tennessee Mountains*. It was printed in 1885 and they only want a couple of dollars for it. I'm a sucker for old books, so I bring it up to the counter and Ivy, the woman behind the counter, says, "Oh, I didn't know we had this," confirming my theory about secondhand bookstores: even the owners can discover books they didn't know about sometimes. "I'd love to read this book. I wish I didn't have to sell it!" Acting on a whim, I decide this is a good time to learn a little more about the character of the town. "Tell you what," I say. "I'll pay for the book, and I'll throw in a few dollars for shipping and leave you my card. You keep the book and read it, and mail it to me when you're done." She thinks this is a fine idea. I hand her my card and my money and we walk out.

A few weeks later I got the book, along with a kind note. Ivy explained that the dialogue was written in Tennessee mountain dialect, and was simply too much trouble to "decode." The mountains have their own language, one that doesn't always make sense to those who dwell at their feet. She gave up on the book, and she's sent it with her best wishes and hopes that I could decode it more easily.

My experiment proved to be quite satisfactory, and if ever I get back to Tellico Plains, I'll be sure to look up Ivy at The Bookshelf. Like Mark, and the woman at the Green Cove Motel, she seems like a good soul, the sort of person one wants as a neighbor, no matter where you live. But I've decided that the book deserved to go out of print. It wasn't all that interesting a book, and it didn't have a thing to say about trout.

Conclusion

Downstream

David O'Hara

I believe that the most loving thing you can say to a person is "Look." And the most loving stance is not a close embrace, but two people standing side by side, looking out together on the world. When people learn to look, they begin to see, really see. When they begin to see, they begin to care. And caring is the portal into the moral world.

—Kathleen Dean Moore, *The Pine Island Paradox*

Someone once pointed out to me that the Bible begins in Eden and ends in the new Jerusalem. As someone who loves the outdoors, the idea that "progress" leads from a garden to a city isn't all that appealing. If heaven is a city, I think I'd rather live—and fish—in the mountains beyond its suburbs.

I've found some consolation in discovering another way to think about it: the setting may change from garden to city, but one thing remains consistent in those stories from Genesis and Revelation. Regardless of the setting, the places are refreshed by rivers flowing through them. No matter where we live, our lives are made better by flowing water.

I work in the city of Sioux Falls, a city named for falling water. I'm fairly certain that the people who named it knew that the word *falls* is a word that draws settlers. Sioux Falls is in Minnehaha County, which gets its

126

name from the Lakota word for waterfall. *Minne* means "water," and *haha* means (not surprisingly) "laughing." When a river falls over rocks, when it is free to run and frolic and plunge, it laughs. There's probably some ancient genetic memory of waters that makes us feel the laughter of a brook and make it our own. Standing in the waters of a stream refreshes the soul. No doubt the ancient writers of the Bible felt the same way. We know some of them were fishermen, and even if they weren't brook trout fishermen, they knew.

My colleagues and friends who do not fish often ask me why I do. There are many reasons, of course. Sometimes I fish for food, but that's not the main reason. Usually I fish in search of other things, like the vital encounter with the fish, the discipline and delight of the pursuit, the hard but rewarding work of clambering upstream, over fallen logs and tall rocks. I fish in order to know the world I live in and, in a sense, to know my own life better. Rivers are places of discovery. Once, while fishing in Vermont, I found an old iron tool once used to shear sheep. It was buried in the mud of the riverbank, and it was nearly disintegrated by years of rusting in the river. Near Middlebury runs the Lemon Fair River, whose name is a corruption of the name given to it by early French settlers, christening it for the mountains from which it flowed, *les monts verts*, the Green Mountains. Vermont earned its nickname, "The Green Mountain State," not from the trees that blanket its mountains but from the sheep pastures that once covered those same hills. Centuries ago much of the state was deforested for those pastures. Stone walls now run through dense hardwood forests throughout the state, markers of forgotten fields that have been succeeded by maple trees that give the state its fall colors and its sweet syrup. Looking at those colors in October, one can imagine that the mountains are as they have always been; it is easy to forget how much we have altered the places we live. And, of course, the places we live, and the things that we do, change us, too. Walking in the river reminds me again of that sentence from Heraclitus: all things are in flux, all things flow and change.

Just as there are many reasons why we fish, there are many reasons why we read. One of the pleasures of reading old books is the delight of brushing up against unfamiliar words. I was reading a text recently that used the word *cubit*. In case you've forgotten, a cubit is a unit of measurement, roughly the length of a man's arm from his elbow to the tip of his fingers. It was once a very useful measurement. Like the foot, the handbreadth, and the inch (based on the length of the first joint of the thumb), it's a measurement you always carry with you. To paraphrase the ancient sophist Protagoras, your body—your very life—thus becomes the measurement of all things. Still, it's not hard to see why a scientific age like ours no longer measures things in cubits. They're too imprecise, since we all have different arms. We want something outside ourselves by which to measure the world. Something steady, something that will always stay the same even as our hands grow and change. Something that doesn't depend on us.

But is there anything that isn't related to us? Matthew and I, in researching and writing this book, have tried to be objective students of these mountains and of their fish, but it was, as we said, our curiosity that prompted us in the first place. Our heads have tried to correlate the data, but it was our hearts that led us here. We have not been impartial students, despite our efforts. We must confess: we love this land, these watersheds, these fish. But if passion were enough for preservation, then none of the lovely things in the world would ever face danger. Sadly, this is not enough. We all live downstream of one another. Donne is right: no man an island. Today we know this truth applies to all species—no member of an ecosystem is completely independent of the other members. A biologist recently pointed out to me that the introduction of lake trout in one watershed in Yellowstone has affected the native cutthroats in other watersheds. The lake trout eat the cutthroats in such quantities that the grizzlies that used to feed on the cutthroats in that watershed now have to seek protein elsewhere, so they're feeding on more elk. Since they eat more elk, the elk browse less along the banks of other streams, making for better streamside cover and less erosion on those streams, and improving that cutthroat habitat. Unfortunately, altering habitats doesn't always work out well. And it is very difficult to take the long view, to see all the consequences of our actions. We act with limited vision. Like men walking in caves with candles, we see the path ahead lit only very dimly. It's never completely obvious what the downstream effects are, and we don't mean to be alarmist. The common ways our species interacts with rivers—dams, for instance—aren't by themselves good or evil. They're a part of our landscape, a part of our lives. But we think there's a lot to be said for knowing something about them.

We change our landscape, and not all change is bad, just as not all change is good. At the risk of offering a tautology, it is what it is. We've written because we want to acknowledge what is, and we want to continue to get to know what is better (or worse) with each year we're given to live here. Before Europeans arrived, Manhattan Island was a wooded island covered with streams and ponds. In those streams, brook trout used to swim. Those streams are now buried under the streets, and it seems unlikely that brook trout will ever swim there again. Brookies are beautiful, marked with the fingerprints of Manitou. When I walk the streets of Manhattan I sometimes think of the ghosts of those ancient trout swimming beneath my feet, and I feel a pang of sadness at their loss. But then again, I admit I'm fond of Manhattan, too.

Those ancient stories of Eden and the heavenly city appeal to us in strange ways, even perhaps for those of us who do not take them literally. In a world in flux, those places stand for the desire to stand some place that will not shift, to find rest in a place that will remain steady forever. Of course, such places are inaccessible to us here and now. Surprisingly, we seek the same peace not just in high and solid places, but in rivers.

There's an old hymn that speaks of "peace like a river." Perhaps this is the other face of Heraclitus's coin: yes, you can never step into the same river twice, but on the other hand, the river is always there. The waters slip by, the seasons change, the ecosystem and its inhabitants evolve, but all the time, the waters flow down, falling with the sound of laughter. The prophet Amos called for justice to flow like a river, words Dr. King echoed during the civil rights struggle in the 1960s. The ancient Greek mapmakers thought our world must be surrounded by a great river they called "Okeanos," from which we get our word *ocean*. In every direction, we eventually come to water. Our lives are bounded by waters. Maybe the biblical writers were right to bound their text with waters as well. According to Genesis, four rivers flow out of Eden. I like to think at least one of them had decent trout. The same goes for the river in the new Jerusalem. Maybe one fine day in the hereafter we will find, swimming in those waters, the brookies displaced from Manhattan. Until then, Matthew and I will continue to look for them in the Appalachians, doing all we can to know them better and to ensure that these fish, touched by the fingers of Manitou, have clean water to swim in. All of this is in flux, we know. We cannot make rivers stay as they are. But we can try to know them not just as resources but as the children of Eden and as the shadows of heaven, places of refreshment and peace where our ancestors drank and where, God willing, so will our children.

Afterword

Bill McKibben

THIS IS A VERY fine book.

It is about fishing, which is not something I do. But the fishing is described so well that I could understand its appeal.

More, though, it's a book about place, or places: about the cool and shaded waters of the upland East, those Appalachian rivers and streams where the native brook trout hold their own, for now. "One of the goals of this book was to connect rivers to people and landscapes and stories of Appalachia," writes Matthew Dickerson—a connection that might begin to heal the ruinous loss of place that lets us regard all spots as essentially the same (if they have good cell phone reception).

The authors encounter the ultimate in that kind of thinking when they reach Kentucky, where state officials insist, dubiously, that there never were any native brook trout (if true, Kentucky would be unique among Appalachian states in that regard). Why might that be? Well, just maybe because the need to protect a pesky species that enjoys clean water might interfere with the coal industry's ongoing project of mountaintop removal. Kentucky really has turned that corner of the commonwealth into a non-place, the mountains made low and the valleys raised up.

But not every story is sad. There are waters coming back to life as well, places where dams have been removed, where citizens have restored drainages and watersheds, where enough notice has been taken of place that place has begun to thrive again. One of the happiest developments of recent decades has been the rise of the Riverkeeper network, beginning on the Hudson but now spreading to rivers (and bays and lakes and the like) across the country. I've been on boats with a dozen of these men and women in various locales, often along the ignored urban stretches of rivers with their weedy, trashy banks. But they're coming back to life, place after place after place.

This gentle book is no activist's tract. It's better than that, by far. It bears witness to what we have right now, the beauty that surrounds all of us who live in the rural East. It bears witness to the stories of these places in the past, and to their possibilities for the future. The prose is calm, composed, and strong: appropriately, there's a strong and deep current that runs through the book, a current of care. It swept me along, start to finish.

Endnotes

1. John Steinbeck, *The Log from the Sea of Cortez* (New York: Penguin, 1995) 2.

2. J. R. R. Tolkien, *The Two Towers; Being the Second Part of* The Lord of the Rings, 2nd ed. (Boston: Houghton Mifflin, 1965) Book IV, Chapter 2.

3. Michael Polanyi, *Personal Knowledge* (New York: Harper & Row, 1964) 55.

4. Ibid., 59.

5. Nick Karas, *Brook Trout* (New York: Lyons, 1997) vii.

6. Craig Nova, after writing several novels, felt compelled to write *Brook Trout and the Writing Life* (New York: Lyons, 1999). There he speaks of the way trout fishing requires one to enter into a transaction with the water; the angler who does not watch the water will not learn from it and will not be able to fish. In describing the places he fishes, Nova writes, "There is nothing vague about these places" (82). The places one fishes are full of determinacy, and yet it is precisely these places in which chance erupts. Nova moves seamlessly between speaking about the fishing to speaking about Camus and Emerson, because the two endeavors, fishing and philosophy, are intimately wedded. Describing a story a friend told him, he says, "Like all fishing stories, it is about the difference between appearance and reality" (79). The characters in his stories have no need for the technical language of philosophy to describe this, though. As one of them puts it, "catching brook trout put him in touch with some 'pretty big things'" (86). Nova nevertheless spells it out for us a little more clearly, though still not with precision: "The frankly unknowable comes into play, and this naturally leads to humility and the contemplation of the infinite" (92).

7. Henry David Thoreau, *A Week on the Concord and Merrimack Rivers* (New York: Signet, 1961) 39.

8. Nova, *Brook Trout and the Writing Life*, 23.

9. C. S. Lewis, *The Collected Letters of C. S. Lewis*, Vol. 1, *Family Letters, 1905–1931*, edited by Walter Hooper (San Francisco: HarperSanFrancisco, 2004) 909.

10. Jimmy Jacobs, *Trout Streams of Southern Appalachia* (Woodstock, VT: Backcountry, 1994) 87.

11. Various Experts with Rod and Reel, *The Speckled Brook Trout (Salvelinus Fontinalis)*, edited and illustrated by Louis Rhead. (New York: R. H. Russell, 1902) 6, "Distribution."

12. Wendell Berry, "A Native Hill," in *The Art of the Commonplace: The Agrarian Essays of Wendell Berry*, edited by Norman Wirzba (Berkeley: Counterpoint, 2002) 15, 18.

13. "Draft Programmatic Environmental Impact Statement (DEIS) on Mountaintop Mining/Valley Fill in Appalachia: Executive Summary," http://www.epa.gov/region03/

mtntop/pdf/executivesummary.pdf, accessed 6/5/2014.

14. G. Pond, et al., "Downstream Effects of Mountaintop Coal Mining: Comparing Biological Conditions Using Family- and Genus-Level Macroinvertebrate Bioassessment Tools," *Journal of the North American Benthological Society* 27 (2008) 717–37.

15. Ibid.

16. Aristotle, *De Generatione et corruptione*, in *Basic Works of Aristotle* (New York: Random House, 1941) 316a5–10.

17. The philosopher Henry Bugbee has a mystical existentialist account of trout fishing that derives as much from his reading of Heidegger and Marcel as it does from his long experience in the trout streams of New England and Montana. I include it here as an endnote because it is relevant to my point, although not directly so. I am arguing in this section that in fishing we come to know the natural environment in a way that we would not know it otherwise, but I have in mind here something like the knowledge that the amateur ecologist has, not unlike that of the devoted birdwatcher. Bugbee argues that the knowledge that comes through intensity of experience on a river is even more profound than that. Knowledge of the river, as it is gained by the fisher, becomes knowledge of the self and of reality itself. It is in some sense for Bugbee the defining moment in reality, the place where we enframe reality and conceive it in our consciousness. Until we fish, the river and the trout are, in some important sense, not really there. When the fish rises and one receives it, one finds that one has already prepared oneself to receive it; the act of fishing is the act of preparing oneself to receive the fish as gift, and so the whole river becomes a single moment of giftedness. This is the orientation that Bugbee would cultivate toward all of life; it begins for him in the river, but its value extends to every aspect of the world. He writes, "It takes many, many days to learn of what may and may not be in the river. Let us wade right in and keep fishing where we are, with our fingertips touching the trembling line. It is just in the moment of the leap we both feel and see, when the trout is instantly born, entire, from the flowing river, that reality is knowingly defined." And again: "Now the river is the unborn, and the sudden fish is just the new-born—whole, entire, complete, individual, and universal. The fisherman may learn that each instant is pregnant with the miracle of the new-born fish, and fishing in the river may become a knowing of each fish even before it is born. As he fishes the ever-flowing current, it teaches him of the fish even before it is born, just in so far as this alert fishing involves 'abiding in no-abode,' or the 'unattached mind.' If one is steeped in the flowing river and sensitized through the trembling line, one anticipates the new-born fish at every moment. The line tautens and with all swiftness, the fish is there, sure enough! And now, in the leaping of this fish, how wonderfully, laughingly clear everything becomes! If eventually one lands it, and kneels beside its silvery form at the water's edge, on the fringe of the gravel bar, if one receives this fish as purely as the river flows, everything is momently given, and the very trees become eloquent where they stand." See Bugbee, *The Inward Morning* (Athens: University of Georgia Press, 1999) 86–87, 130.

18. Ian Frazier gives a similar account of this moment, speaking of "an odd emotional state that sometimes sweeps through me after I catch a big fish. I hold the fish in the shallows and move it gently to revive it and I talk to it and I get dizzy with the sensation of being in a moment that neither of us will forget.... And I feel scarily close to the fish's complex life that went on before and that will go on after.... Seconds pass; we realize we are no longer attached.... the fish swims away." See Frazier, *The Fish's Eye* (New York: Picador, 2002) 73.

19. In Izaak Walton's classic *The Compleat Angler*, Piscator, the angler, attributes this

saying to "An ingenious Spaniard": "Rivers and the inhabitants of the watery elements are made for wise men to contemplate and for fools to pass by without consideration." See *The Compleat Angler* (New York: Everyman's Library, 1965) 29.

20. Horace Kephart, a logger from Michigan, in 1901 said this about the forests up the Tellico River.

21. Cf. Kurt D. Fausch, "A Paradox of Trout Invasions in North America," *Biological Invasions* 10 (2008) 685–701.